Techniques

The instructions in this text depend on Grumbacher's fine acrylic colors, brushes and mediums, including extensive use of Whiteblend, Clearblend and Slowblend. These paints and mediums are water-based and non-toxic. If substitutes are used, the results will vary. Whiteblend, Clearblend and Slowblend are special mediums that slow the drying time of acrylic paints and allow even a novice to create beautiful color blends the first time. They make painting with acrylics wonderfully easy, and you will need them throughout this series. Use only cool, clean water when mixing, painting or cleaning up with these paints and mediums—not oils, thinners or turpentine.

Grumbacher Wet Palette

This is the best way to keep acrylics wet on the palette for as long as you choose, letting you use paint that was mixed hours or even days before. Saturate the sponge pad with water until it almost floats in the tray. Wet both sides of the special paper, place it on the pad and remove any puddles or wrinkles.

Place your paints on the palette paper and mix your colors. The paint will stay workable as long as the sponge pad remains wet. As the pad dries out around the edges, the paper will curl. When this happens, lift up a corner of the paper, pour water over the pad and press the paper back in place. Place the lid on the tray when you need to store mixed paints.

Mixing Colors

Mixing colors, like painting, is an art—not a science! It's up to you to decide exact hues; there are no exact formulas. The color mixtures in this book are based on Grumbacher Artists' Acrylics. Colors are listed in order of the quantity used; some approximate proportions are given. Often it's best to mix colors directly on the brush or sponge. This is particularly useful when only a small amount is needed or when a gradual change of value or color is desired, as when highlighting an object.

All the projects in this book require some colors to be prepared before you begin. For these mixtures, squeeze out a marble-sized dollop of each tube pigment required along the edge of your palette paper. Use a clean painting knife to pull a small amount (about the size of a pea) of the first pigment from the dollop. Add other colors in lesser amounts and mix to a uniform shade. Mix and adjust the color as needed. It is easier to add color to a mixture than to subtract it, so always start with small portions. When you have determined the right proportions, mix the amount that you think you'll need. Often more paint is required than you expect, and the excess is handy for touchups.

Unless the instructions state otherwise, paint mixtures should have the "creamy" consistency of Whiteblend. Occasionally the instructions will call for a *watery* consistency—add enough water to the paint to give it the density of ink. When instructed to create a *marbleized* mixture, do not mix the paints completely, but rather leave a mottled, streaky appearance as shown at left.

Transferring and Protecting the Design

Select the appropriate pattern from the pullout section of this book. Lay the canvas on a flat, sturdy surface. Refer to the painting instructions to position the pattern, then tape it firmly in place. (Note: The patterns are flexible; you can move the elements around. For example, you can place the birds in "Handouts" anywhere on the canvas, and use more or fewer as you choose.)

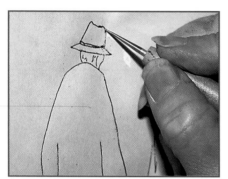

Transferring a pattern

Insert a piece of graphite paper between the pattern and canvas; trace the lines with a stylus or pencil to transfer them. Lift a corner of the graphite paper to see if you missed any lines.

When the directions require an adhesive design protector, use the same technique to trace only the outline onto adhesive paper. Cut out the image, remove the backing and press it onto the canvas.

Applying an adhesive protector

Paint carefully around the adhesive protector. Start with the brush on the cutout area and stroke away from it. If you stroke toward the cutout, you will force paint underneath it.

If transfer lines remain after the painting is finished, dry the area thoroughly and erase the lines with a kneaded eraser or clean moist sponge.

Applying Paints

Familiarize yourself by studying the color placements of the painting. Read through the instructions, visualizing how you are going to execute each step. Have a piece of canvas or a scrap of watercolor paper handy to test your colors and strokes before applying them to the painting. Working **wet-on-wet** is easy. Use a clean, towel-dried brush or sponge and work quickly. Working **wet-on-dry** is easier. Use a clean, moist brush or tool. This technique allows you to work as quickly or as slowly as you desire. Working **wet-on-sticky** is tricky! Add Clearblend or Slowblend to the sticky area of paint, allow the paint to dry thoroughly, then touch up with a wet-over-dry technique.

Removing the protector after painting

Loading the brushes: Keep a large container of clean water nearby, and always moisten your brushes before using them. Before loading them with paint, remove excess water from large brushes by squeezing the bristles. Tap smaller brushes on a clean towel. If you do not get good coverage, moisten the brush again.

Double loading: This refers to applying two colors to the brush at one time. It is easier for creating delicate details such as birds or tree limbs, as shown at left. Load the brush with the darkest color of the subject matter. Pull one side of the brush through the highlight color to create a dark and a light side. Position the brush so the stroke will be half dark and half light as you draw it along the canvas.

Loading a painting knife: Use the knife to spread the paint in a thin layer across the palette. Remove the paint from the knife. Hold the knife edge in the paint and pull back diagonally to load a ribbon of paint along the edge.

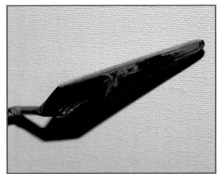

Blending colors: Apply each color quickly and generously, overlapping them at least ½". Use a clean, towel-dried brush and work over the overlapped area with elongated figure-8 strokes, frequently wiping the excess paint off the brush. When the colors are mingled, blend with long strokes, brushing back and forth. Begin blending with firm pressure; use a feather touch for the finishing strokes.

Pat-blending: Load the brush generously with Clearblend, lightly wiping off the excess on a paper towel. Apply the highlight color with a different brush, then pat and tap with the blending brush to gradually soften the edges into the background color. Don't work too hard to blend the colors smoothly—an irregular look is more natural.

Highlights, shadows and catchlights: Blend lighter color into a highlighted area, darker colors into areas which are shaded. On a smooth, polished surface (such as a bubble or an eye) a highlight has a sharper edge and is called a catchlight. These may simply be dots of a brighter color.

C-strokes: C-strokes are used to create movement or to contour objects such as shells, the bottoms of waves or a bird's feather. Use a short, curving stroke to pull the wet paint into a comma or an elongated "C" shape. Often the stroke is tilted.

Crunching, stippling and tapping: Occasionally the instructions call for you to "crunch" in a color. Hold the loaded brush perpendicular to the canvas and push straight in, fanning the bristles out a bit.

"Stippling" uses the same motion with a little less pressure; "tapping" or "patting" uses even less pressure than stippling.

Use creamy paint, the consistency of Whiteblend, for crunching. Thin the paint slightly for stippling, patting or tapping.

Contrast, perspective and depth: Place dark colors against light and light colors against dark. Darker, more vibrant colors are generally placed in the foreground; lighter, muted colors are applied in the background. Objects of medium value are placed in between.

The more distant the object, the smaller it becomes and the closer it appears to the horizon line. Middle ground objects will be farther from the horizon, larger, and more defined. The foreground objects are lowest on the canvas, largest in size and most sharply focused.

Special Techniques

Skies: Work quickly, blocking in the sky colors with a generous amount of paint. Overlap colors ½" or more. Blend immediately with a clean, towel-dried brush until the desired effect is achieved.

Half-dry skies and backgrounds always look streaked; you may have the urge to overwork them, but don't. Allow them to dry completely. After the painting is finished, you will find that a streak or two in the background or sky is realistic. If the appearance is still unacceptable when dry, touch up with a wet-on-dry technique or paint over it completely.

Reflections and water lines: Water works like a mirror, picking up images and colors around it. Visualize your subject matter sitting on a mirror and paint the reflection accordingly. Keep all predominant strokes horizontal.

Add horizontal water lines to make the reflections appear to be underwater. Load the painting knife with Whiteblend and place the edge against the canvas. Soften the edges with a clean brush moistened with Clearblend. For more coverage, hold the knife at a 45° angle. Reflections can be painted wet-on-wet or added to a dry surface.

Ocean waves: Oceans and waves can be painted either wet-on-wet or wet-on-dry. Apply the basic colors and blend using the wet-on-wet technique.

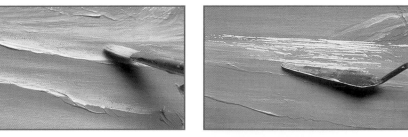

Use a painting knife to paint a tide line, gradually turning the knife flatter on the canvas as you move it across. For distant whitecaps, add a horizontal highlight with either a painting knife or a liner brush. Soften or blend the bottom and side edges with a brush moistened with Clearblend.

Grass: The illusion of grass can be created either wet-on-wet or wet-on-dry. With a variety of tools and different strokes, many different appearances can be achieved.

1 When creating a thick field of grass wet-on-wet, use large gesso brushes. Alternate one brush loaded with light color and another loaded with dark. Hold the brush perpendicular to the canvas and crunch with a slightly upward thrust, but do not allow the bristles to slide upward. Done properly, the brush bristles will arch slightly and the top outer bristles will flare out, creating many irregular lengths of grass blades.

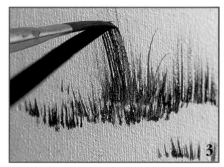

2 Start accenting the foreground grass with a gesso brush, using the least contrasting accent color that will be in that area. A fan brush is more convenient in the distant fields and for final detail in the foreground.

Regardless of the technique used, to avoid bare spots, each additional row should slightly overlap the base of the previous one. Begin with a light color in the distance and end with a dark color at the bottom of the canvas. Add a contrasting patch of color in one area to create additional depth.

An easy way to create field grass wet-on-dry is to basecoat the grass areas with the appropriate colors for your composition, using the darkest colors at the bottom of the canvas. Stipple accent and highlight colors over the dry base coat.

3 Use a Multi-Texture or fan brush for clusters of grass or marsh grass. When instructed to "pull up" or "lift up" the grass blades, use watery paint and stroke the brush upward, using firm pressure at the root and tapering off to very light pressure at the tip until the brush lifts off the canvas.

4 Lift up taller grasses with a liner brush. Work the paint wet-on-wet. Alternating and overlapping light and dark paints will create a variety of colors and values.

All water lines must be flat, so keep the bases of marsh grass rows parallel to the bottom of the canvas.

Foliage: Foliage and foliage highlights can be painted with brushes or sponges, applied wet-on-wet or wet-on-dry. The most widely used brushes for stippling foliage are bristle brushes. The foliage can be dense or sparse, depending on the pressure of application. To create sparse foliage, use light pressure. For dense foliage, use light pressure on the edges but heavier pressure in the center. You can also use a brush or painting knife to fill in the center.

1 To create foliage with a sponge, load a small section with paint and tap irregular leaves on the canvas. While the paint is still wet, pat over it with a moist sponge to texture it.

2 Apply highlights sparsely and use light pressure throughout. To achieve a rounded appearance, tap the canvas lightly. Use less of the color and a lighter touch when applying each highlight; never block out all the base foliage color.

3 Apply the darkest or dullest highlight ¾ of the way around the foliage. Add the middle-value highlight more sparingly, about halfway around the foliage. The brightest highlight is lightly stippled on the front ¼. Any reflected lights are sparingly applied to the darkest, shadowy areas of the foliage.

Drying Your Painting

Acrylics dry at an uneven rate. Often the outer edges of an application begin to dry first. This can cause a spotty appearance when drying, but the color will even out when it is completely dry. Acrylics will be darker when dry than while wet.

Two techniques that will extend a painting's dry time: Moisten the canvas with water before applying paint, or add a few drops of Slowblend or Grumbacher Acrylic Retarder to each tube color on your palette before mixing. Do not add more than one part medium to two parts paint.

Keep a hair dryer handy when you paint—it can save you a lot of time between steps. Hold the hair dryer a few inches away from the canvas. Use a low temperature and keep moving it around the canvas.

Signing Your Painting

Stand back and look over your painting. Believe it or not, it will be even more beautiful tomorrow! You can sign your painting with watery acrylic paint or a Koh-I-Noor Rapidograph pen.

After your painting is completed and signed, let it dry thoroughly, then use a kneaded eraser to remove any remaining pencil or graphite paper lines. Varnish it with Grumbacher Acrylic Painting Varnish or with Matte Medium.

Cleaning Your Brushes

Wipe excess paint off your brushes with a rag, then wash them with Grumbacher Brush Soap and cool, clean tap water. The soap container has a ridged cleaning surface. Lather the brush and lightly scrub it on the grid. Rinse; towel dry. This will clean and condition the brushes at the same time. Allow them to dry flat to avoid bent bristles.

Dry paint can be removed from brushes or other areas with alcohol. Denatured alcohol works best. If a brush is hard with acrylic paint, you may need to soak it for a few minutes before attempting to remove the paint. Be careful with the alcohol—it can remove the finish from some furniture!

Correcting Mistakes

Are you afraid of making a mistake while painting? Don't be! Know up front that you will make a mistake occasionally. We all do. No matter how long you paint or how masterful you become as an artist, you will make a mistake from time to time. The only people not making mistakes are those people who are doing nothing at all.

Anything you put on your canvas can be corrected. If it is wet, you simply wipe it off. If dry, you can scrub it off with a toothbrush moistened with Slowblend. For tougher jobs, use a wire brush from the hardware store, or simply paint over it!

Because acrylics dry quickly, it is best to stop and fix obvious errors as they occur. Keep a clean, damp sponge handy to wipe them out. It is also best to dry your painting thoroughly between steps; then errors will simply wipe off, leaving the dry paint undisturbed.

If you have painted a "fat" limb or a crooked line, you know it right away. Use a clean, moist angle brush to push excess paint back into the line or remove it.

If you have really goofed—and the goofy thing has dried—you can still fix the painting. If it is a mistake covering a large area, just paint over it. Train yourself to think creatively! Could you cover it with foliage or a cloud?

The best source of correcting techniques is to view them as they are demonstrated in my workshops. Hope to see you there! Now, let's paint!

Cherry Blossom Time

Grumbacher Acrylic Colors
Burnt Umber
Cadmium Yellow Medium
Grumbacher Payne's Gray
Grumbacher Red (Naphthol Red)
Prussian Blue
Thalo® Blue
Thalo® Crimson
Thalo® Yellow Green
Titanium White
Ultramarine Blue

Brushes
Two 2" Gesso Brushes
2" Hake Brush
#1 Bristle Fan Brush
Eterna #12 Round Bristle Brush
Gainsborough® #6 Flat Bristle Brush
½" Sable Essence™ Angle Brush
Golden Edge™ #2 Liner Brush
Multi-Texture Brush

Other Supplies
16"x20" Stretched Canvas
Grumbacher Acrylic Painting Varnish
Whiteblend
Clearblend
Natural Sponge
Black Graphite Paper
Stylus

Palette
Before you begin, prepare these color mixtures:

Medium Violet-Gray—6 parts Whiteblend, 1 part Ultramarine Blue, 1 part Grumbacher Payne's Gray, touch of Thalo® Crimson

Light Violet-Gray—6 parts Whiteblend, 1 part Medium Violet-Gray

Medium Blue—4 parts Whiteblend, 4 parts Prussian Blue, 1 part Thalo® Crimson

Grass highlight—2 parts Whiteblend, 1 part Medium Blue, 1 part Thalo® Yellow Green

Lime Green—1 part Thalo® Yellow Green, l part Whiteblend

Light Yellow—10 parts Whiteblend, 1 part Cadmium Yellow Medium

Teal—Whiteblend, touch of Thalo® Blue

Rose—1 part Thalo® Crimson, 1 part Whiteblend

Rose Highlight—Rose, Titanium White

Pink—Whiteblend, touch of Grumbacher Red

Pink Highlight—Pink, Titanium White

Smoke—marbleized Burnt Umber, touch of Medium Violet-Gray

Salmon—marbleized Whiteblend, Pink, Light Yellow

1 Measuring from the bottom of the canvas, sketch the design so the top of the most distant hill on the right is 7", the most distant water edge is 3½" and the foremost water edge is 1½" from the bottom. On the left side, the top of the most distant hill is 6¾" up, the middle hill 6" and the foremost 5¼" up. Using a very moist 2" gesso brush, cover the sky area down to the most distant meadow line generously with Whiteblend. While the Whiteblend is wet, brush-mix a touch of Prussian Blue into the uncleaned brush and use a figure-8 stroke to randomly apply cloud formations in the center sky. Reload the brush as needed, but do not cover all the white.

1

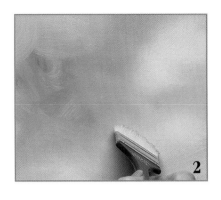

2 While the paint is still wet, blend with an erratic motion of the hake brush. Towel-clean the hake often during the blending process.

3 With the round bristle brush and light violet-gray, tap in the distant tree line. Brush-mix a touch of grass highlight and violet-gray and lightly tap it around in the distant trees.

4 For the three rolling meadows behind the water, work wet-into-wet, creating a gradual transition of value in each hill and the overall area. With a flat bristle brush, apply Whiteblend along the crest and light violet-gray in the bottom or valley of the most distant hill. Blend. While this is wet, use a fan brush lightly loaded with grass highlight to highlight the hill. Starting in the white area, hold the fan brush almost flat against the canvas, with the handle pointing down, and "flap" it against the canvas. Add lime to the uncleaned brush and apply lighter highlights along the hill in the center of the canvas. Create the middle hill in the same way, but use medium violet-gray in the valley.

5 For the valley, or foremost part of the hill nearest the water, use medium blue. Apply this paint so that it extends slightly into the water's edge.

6 Use the sponge with medium violet-gray to apply the top section of foliage along the right side of the canvas. Tap the sponge lightly to create loose, leafy edges, harder for more solid foliage. Add medium blue to the sponge for the slightly darker lower portions.

7 Tap with grass highlight on the fan brush to add highlights below the foliage and across the canvas. Add lime and lime brush-mixed with light yellow in the brightest areas.

8 Use smoke on the flat bristle brush to apply the rocks along the distant water edge.

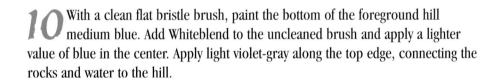

9 Use a clean flat bristle brush and teal to apply the waterfall around the center of the water area. Add medium blue to the uncleaned brush, paint the remainder of the water area so that it overlaps the bottom edge of the meadow slightly, and blend. Add streaks of teal in the water. Add rocks along the foremost water edge as before.

10 With a clean flat bristle brush, paint the bottom of the foreground hill medium blue. Add Whiteblend to the uncleaned brush and apply a lighter value of blue in the center. Apply light violet-gray along the top edge, connecting the rocks and water to the hill.

11 Continue while the paint is still wet. Look at the finished painting for placement of the shadows and highlights. Use a gesso brush with smoke to crunch a shadow in the grass where the trees will later be planted. Crunch speckles of three highlight values on the foremost hill. Apply the highlights along the crest of the hill with flapping and crunching strokes of the fan brush. For the center and lower areas of the hill, apply the highlights with crunching strokes of the gesso brush. With clean brushes, apply the first, dullest highlight of grass highlight. Apply a second, middle-value highlight of grass highlight brush-mixed with lime green in the center of the hill. For the lightest highlights, add light yellow to the uncleaned brush and apply only in the brightest areas. Do not paint too solidly—allow the base colors to show through the highlights. Should the highlights become solid, clean the brush and crunch the area with the appropriate base color. Dry.

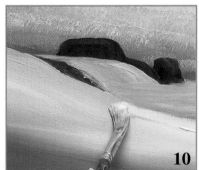

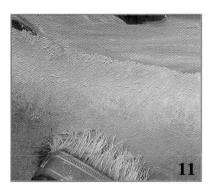

12 With grass highlight on the round bristle brush, highlight the top right sides of the foliage on the right side of the canvas. Add lime to the uncleaned brush and add a brighter top edge to the low foliage. With the fan brush and the grass highlight colors, touch up the grass where needed by lightly crunching in contrasting colors.

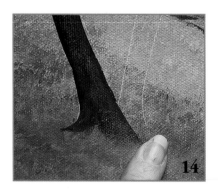

13 With the angle brush and smoke, reshape the rocks and add additional rocks if needed. Cover the rocks with Clearblend. Use a clean angle brush with salmon to highlight the tops and right sides. Blend or soften the edge of the salmon with a clean angle brush moistened with Clearblend.

14 Paint the tree trunks and main limbs with the angle brush and smoke. Immediately blot the bases and roots of the wet tree paint to "plant" the tree.

15 Use the angle brush with salmon to highlight the trunks. Hold the brush vertically, making short downward strokes to create a choppy bark texture.

16 With the liner brush and a watery mixture of smoke, apply the limbs coming off the tree trunks. Use a liner double loaded with smoke and salmon to add a few more limbs. To create a taper at the tips of the limbs, apply less pressure on the brush as you pull away from the tree.

17 Use the Multi-Texture brush lightly loaded with Whiteblend to apply highlight streaks on the waterfall.

18 Use a fan brush moistened with Clearblend to cover the water area. While it is wet, add horizontal waterlines and ripples with the Multi-Texture brush and Whiteblend. Soften or blend the bottoms and side edges of the Whiteblend. Crunch a few splashes in the water area next to the base of the rocks with the fan brush and Whiteblend. Soften the bottoms and edges with a clean fan or multi-texture brush. Add a few more rocks at the base of the waterfall. When the rocks are dry, add the splashes.

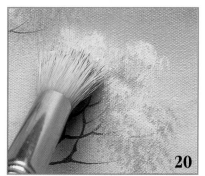

19 Use a sponge or large round bristle brush with medium violet-gray to apply sparse clusters of foliage on the trees. Add medium blue to the uncleaned brush and apply to the left sides of the trees. Brush-mix rose and medium violet-gray with the large round bristle brush, then add shadowy cherry blossoms in the tree foliage and on the short shrubs behind the water at the right side of the canvas. With the fan brush, tap fallen flower petals of the same color in the grass. Blot the bottom of the wet shadowy flower color frequently as you apply it to create soft transitions.

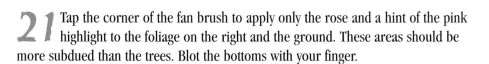

20 With a clean large round bristle brush and rose, highlight the top and right edges of the tree clusters; add a bit in the grass. Add a touch of Titanium White to the uncleaned brush for a few lighter blooms. Repeat with pink.

21 Tap the corner of the fan brush to apply only the rose and a hint of the pink highlight to the foliage on the right and the ground. These areas should be more subdued than the trees. Blot the bottoms with your finger.

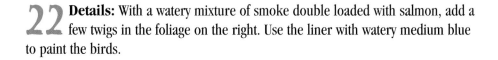

22 **Details:** With a watery mixture of smoke double loaded with salmon, add a few twigs in the foliage on the right. Use the liner with watery medium blue to paint the birds.

Sign and take a stroll down "cherry lane." When your painting is completely dry, use a kneaded eraser or moist sponge to remove any pencil or graphite lines, then spray it with Grumbacher Acrylic Painting Varnish.

Where Eagles Dare

Brushes · Supplies

Grumbacher Acrylic Colors
Burnt Umber
Cadmium Yellow Medium
Monoazo Orange
Prussian Blue
Ultramarine Blue

Brushes
Two 2" Gesso Brushes
#1 Bristle Fan Brush
2" Hake Brush
Eterna #6 or #8 Flat Bristle Brush
Sable Essence™ ½" Angle Brush
Golden Edge™ #2 Liner Brush
Professional™ #6 Bristle Filbert Brush
Golden Edge™ #6 Round Brush

Other Supplies
16"x20" Stretched Canvas
Grumbacher Acrylic Painting Varnish
Whiteblend
Clearblend
Slowblend
Tapered Painting Knife
Natural Sponge

Palette
Before you begin, prepare these color mixtures:

Sky Blue—1 part Ultramarine Blue, 3 parts Whiteblend, touch of Burnt Umber

Pale Pink—Whiteblend, touch of Monoazo Orange

Dark Blue-Green—5 parts Prussian Blue, touch of Burnt Umber

Values of Dark Blue-Green—Dark Blue-Green, Whiteblend

Marbleized Peach—Whiteblend, Monoazo Orange, Cadmium Yellow Medium

1 **Canvas preparation:** Draw a horizon line 4" from the bottom of the canvas. Thoroughly wet the back of the canvas with clean water and let it remain face down for a few minutes to soak in. Dampen the front. Blot excess drips and runs just before applying paint. **Sky base:** Use a gesso brush with pale pink to generously paint the sky area from the top of the canvas to the horizon line. Wipe excess paint from the brush, then paint sky blue horizontally across the top of the wet sky, gradually moving down with each stroke and fading to pale pink about halfway down. Blend with a clean, towel-dried gesso brush if needed.

1

2 While the sky is still wet, use the uncleaned brush to apply cloud shadows with a variety of blue-green values. Scrub the color on quickly, using one corner of the brush in an erratic circular stroke. First mix a small amount of blue-green into the uncleaned brush to create a light value and apply the top clouds. Add more blue-green to the uncleaned brush and continue, making each lower cloud darker in value. Repeat until all the upper clouds are applied. (If the base color becomes sticky and unworkable before all the clouds are done, dry and proceed as described in step 5, alternate method.)

3 Use circular strokes of a fan brush to reshape and blend the clouds' edges. Add a few drifting clouds throughout the sky. Use the hake brush for final blending and for smoothing away brush marks. Use a feather-like touch and clean the brush frequently during the blending process.

4 Wet again and add more pink to the bottom of the sky. Dry the canvas thoroughly.

5 Paint the lower clouds as before; leave a 3" strip of unpainted canvas above the water line. With a clean, towel-dried gesso brush, blend the bottom of the lowest cloud to create a gradual transition and a light glow above the water line. (*Alternate method, wet-on-dry: Moisten the area in which you plan to apply the next cloud, including the bottom of the dry cloud above it, with Clearblend. Use a mixture of pale pink and blue-green to shape the cloud formation. Fade and blend the top of the cloud over the bottom of the one above it along the canvas edges. Use a clean brush moistened with Clearblend for this if needed. Moisten the bottom cloud area with Clearblend. Apply a 4" strip of pale pink at the horizon.*

6 *Apply appropriate values of blue-green to create the top area of the bottom cloud formation. Blend the bottom of the darkest, lowest cloud into the wet pink paint, creating a glow above the horizon. Connect the low cloud to the above clouds on both sides of the canvas with a clean brush moistened with Clearblend.)*

7 Water: Use the flat brush to apply pale pink in the center of the water area. Clean the brush. Apply dark blue-green below the water line and along the bottom of the canvas, overlapping the edges of the pink. Blend with horizontal strokes of a clean fan brush. Add short horizontal streaks of marbleized peach in the center of the light pink area and blend. Dry.

8 Cloud highlights: Observe the finished sky and note the placement of the highlights. Work one area at a time, frequently cleaning and reloading the brush. Load marbleized peach on one corner of the fan brush and Whiteblend on the other. Load the filbert with Clearblend and lightly blot excess on a paper towel. Alternately and randomly tap tiny amounts of peach and Whiteblend onto the top right edge of a cloud.

9 Immediately, while it is still wet, use a moist filbert brush to pat-blend the bottom of the paint down into the cloud until it gradually disappears. Stagger your "pats," leaving irregular spaces, to create a rolling, puffy appearance. Apply more paint and repeat until you are satisfied. Reload and blot the filbert brush frequently while blending. Remove any unwanted highlights with a clean moist sponge. Highlight the cloud centers and pat-blend.

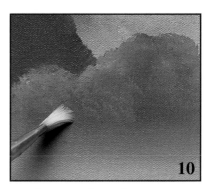

10 Use the same technique to highlight the dark bottom cloud with a lighter value of blue-green (don't use peach and white here). Pat the bottom until it disappears.

11 Trees: Use the fan and flat bristle brushes with dark blue-green to apply the distant trees. Create irregular shapes by alternating brush and brush angles, turning them first horizontally, then vertically as you tap.

12 Use the liner brush with Burnt Umber and a touch of watery dark blue-green to apply the trunk on the left side. Add a highlight of marbleized peach randomly along the trunk.

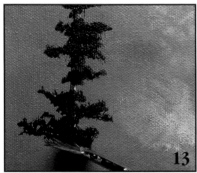

13 Stagger the foliage along the trunk, using the corner of the fan brush in a light tapping motion, allowing the tree trunk to show through.

14 Add Cadmium Yellow Medium and a touch of Whiteblend to the uncleaned fan brush for the highlights on the foreground tree. Apply on the tops of limbs about ⅔ of the way around. For the distant foliage, use the same colors on a flat or filbert brush. Apply to the top and right edges of each clump and about ¾ the way around each. Add more Cadmium Yellow Medium and Whiteblend to create a bright yellow-green final highlight. Apply it sparingly and only to the top and outer edges of some clumps and the right side of the tall tree.

15 Use the flat brush to brush-mix sky blue and dark blue-green; tap this color around the shadows of the dark blue-green foliage.

16 **Rocks and reflections:** Use the angle brush to mix marbleized dark blue-green and Burnt Umber to paint the rocks. Use a fan brush with Clearblend to cover the water area beneath the rocks on the left. While it is wet, use a flat bristle brush to paint a translucent mirror image of the rock directly below it.

17 With a clean angle or flat brush and peach, highlight the top right edges of the rocks and reflections. Fade the highlight edges into the rocks.

18 With a clean fan brush, brush horizontally from the right and the left over the wet reflection to create shimmers in the water. Clean the brush between strokes. Dry.

19 Moisten the rocks with Clearblend. Add alternate highlights of peach and pink; add additional highlights along the right edges of the rocks on the left of the canvas. Fade the edges with a clean angle brush moistened with Clearblend. Add reflected lights on the left sides of the rocks with brush-mixed dark blue-green and Whiteblend. Highlight the right edges with peach.

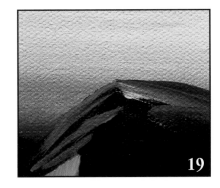

20 With the painting knife lightly loaded with a medium value of blue-green, apply reflected light in the dark water areas. With a clean fan brush moistened with Clearblend, brush horizontally over the color, fading to create shimmer in the water.

21 Double load the liner with Burnt Umber and peach. Apply tree trunks and rocks in the distant tree area.

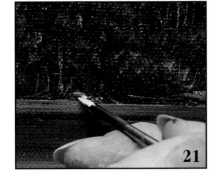

22 With a liner and watery values of dark to light blue-green, add the foreground grasses. Dry.

23 **Eagles:** Transfer the eagles so that the heads and tails are in a dark area of the sky. Using the liner or round brush, paint the wings Burnt Umber. Apply the heads and tails with Whiteblend and shadow with sky blue. Brush-mix Cadmium Yellow Medium with a touch of Whiteblend to paint the beaks.

Sign and soar "where eagles dare!" After your painting is completely dry, use a kneaded eraser or damp sponge to remove any transfer marks, then spray it with Grumbacher Acrylic Picture Varnish.

Bandit

Grumbacher Acrylic Colors
Burnt Sienna
Burnt Umber
Chromium Oxide Green
Grumbacher Payne's Gray
Grumbacher Purple (Dioxazine Purple)
Mars Black
Titanium White
Ultramarine Blue
Yellow Ochre Light

Brushes
2" Gesso Brush
Golden Edge™ #2 Liner Brush
½" Sable Essence™ Angle Brush
Gainsborough® #6 Flat Bristle Brush
Golden Edge™ #6 Round Brush
Golden Edge™ #8 Filbert Brush
#1 Bristle Fan Brush
Multi-Texture Brush

Other Supplies
16"x20" Stretched Canvas
Grumbacher Acrylic Painting Varnish
Clearblend
Whiteblend
Graphite Paper: Black, White
White Graphite Pencil
Stylus, Pencil
Natural Sponge
Tapered Painting Knife

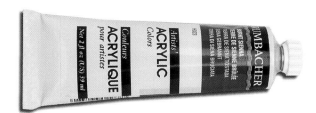

Palette
Before you begin, prepare these color mixtures:

Medium Gray—10 parts Whiteblend, 1 part Mars Black (mix a pancake-sized amount)

Warm Gray—4 parts Medium Gray, 1 part Burnt Sienna, 1 part Whiteblend (brush-mix different values)

Blue-Gray—4 parts medium gray, 1 part Ultramarine Blue, 1 part Whiteblend (brush-mix different values)

Moss Green-Gray—6 parts Medium Gray, Chromium Oxide Green (brush-mix different values)

Light Gray—1 part Medium Gray, 2 parts Whiteblend

Violet-Gray—9 parts Whiteblend, 5 parts Ultramarine Blue, ½ part Burnt Umber, 1½ parts Grumbacher Purple

Shadow—Clearblend, Mars Black, Grumbacher Purple, Ultramarine Blue

Sky Blue—Whiteblend, Ultramarine Blue

Hay Shadow—Grumbacher Purple, Yellow Ochre Light, touch of Whiteblend (brush-mix different values)

Wheat—1 part Yellow Ochre Light, 6 parts Whiteblend (brush-mix additional Whiteblend for lighter values)

Terra Cotta— Burnt Sienna, 1 part Yellow Ochre Light, 1 part Whiteblend

Charcoal—2 parts Burnt Umber, 2 parts Whiteblend, 1 part Mars Black

1 **Canvas preparation:** Mark the door outlines, making a 4" border on the left, 3" on the bottom and 5" on the right. Use a gesso brush and a flat bristle brush with Mars Black to paint inside the door. Paint the rest of the canvas medium gray. Dry. Use white graphite paper to transfer the raccoon. Use a white pencil to draw the barn boards.

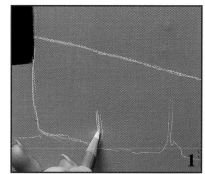

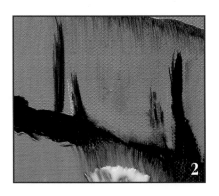

2 **Barn:** Use a gesso brush to apply Clearblend below the door, braces and moldings. While the Clearblend is wet, use the angle or fan brush with shadow to apply the wood cracks and the shadows. With a clean fan brush moistened with Clearblend, stroke the shadow bottoms first down, then horizontally, fading the edges and creating a graduated translucent wash. Clean your blending brush frequently. Dry; repeat if needed.

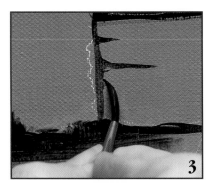

3 Establish separations between boards with the liner brush and watery Mars Black. Inside the barn, indicate light showing between the barn boards with vertical lines of sky blue.

4 Use the liner with various values of hay shadow to swish back and forth, making hay inside the barn around the raccoon. Add hay to the uncleaned brush as you paint closer to the bottom of the canvas. Be loose and erratic with your strokes. Add sky blue to the uncleaned brush and apply a few strokes of reflected light.

5 Double load the angle brush with medium gray and Mars Black to establish the molding edges around the inside of the door. Dry.

6 Unless you're a fast painter, work one section of the barn wood at a time—for example, the wood left of the door, then right of the door, then underneath. Cover a section with Clearblend. While it is wet, use a Multi-Texture or fan brush to apply irregular streaks of warm gray, blue-gray, moss green-gray, and light gray over the base color to indicate variations in the wood. Follow the grain of the wood. Brush-mix and vary the mixtures to create a variety of colors streaking over the base. Thin the paint as needed and do not cover the wood solidly. (The Multi-Texture brush is easier to use on short sections and small spaces.) Subdue some of the bold lines. Tone some of the grays with a Multi-Texture brush loaded with charcoal. Dry.

7 Touch up the bottom and outer edges of the weathered wood with your angular or flat bristle brush using your choice of wood-grain colors. Blend the inside edges of the wet "touch up" paint according to the grain of the wood with Clearblend. Repeat for each area.

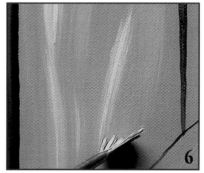

8 Touch up as needed. Add thin, irregular hairline cracks and grooves in the wood with watery shadow on the liner brush. Randomly blot the cracks and grooves with your finger to subdue the detail. Use a fan brush to soften the lines.

9 Use a liner brush with Burnt Sienna to apply the nails and an angle brush with Burnt Sienna for the pulley. Shadow under both with Burnt Umber. Use a liner loaded with brush-mixed Burnt Sienna and Whiteblend to highlight the pulley. Dry. Add Clearblend under the pulley, streak with shadow and blend.

10 Use a fan brush with Clearblend to moisten under the nails and pulley. While the Clearblend is wet, use a liner with watery Burnt Sienna to make rust stains. Immediately brush the bottoms downward with a clean fan brush moistened with Clearblend to fade the lower edges. Make the stains irregular in shape and value.

11 **Eye:** (A) Use a flat detail brush to paint the top Burnt Umber and the bottom Burnt Sienna; blend. (B) Use a liner with watery terra cotta to apply the lines radiating from the center. To make the eye appear convex, use less pressure on the brush as you stroke outward, allowing the lines to taper and disappear before reaching the edge. Dry. (C) Use the liner with Mars Black to paint the pupil. Dry. (D) Cover the eye with Clearblend. While it is wet, add a dot of sky blue at the top and use a clean brush moistened with Clearblend to pat-blend the edges, creating a translucent reflection of the sky. Dry. (E) Apply a catchlight at 11:00. (F) Use the liner brush with watery medium gray to outline the eye socket, skipping around so the outline doesn't appear too solid. Vary the color by brush-mixing Burnt Sienna and Whiteblend into the gray. Touch up with the liner and watery Mars Black as needed. Dry, then erase the graphite circle.

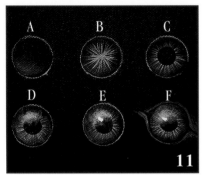

11

12 **Fur:** You may find it easier to turn the canvas—this will allow you to paint with more natural strokes. Create a variety of watery fur colors by brush-mixing them with a Multi-Texture brush, making each layer lighter in value as you progress. Begin with milky charcoal, shaping the body by applying more strokes in the light areas. Apply the fur in the direction and length of growth; note that the fur on the muzzle, face and ears is shorter than the body fur. Tap the brush to create short, stubbly fur; drag it for longer fur. Apply very little pressure on the brush to create thin individual fur marks. Blot the bases of the strokes to "plant" the fur roots. Add Burnt Sienna and a touch of Whiteblend to the uncleaned brush and repeat.

13 Create additional fur values by adding various grays from the barn wood to the uncleaned brush. Don't put light values in shadow areas. As the colors get lighter in value, apply less. Add water to thin the colors to the consistency of milk. Lighten the value of the fur color by adding wheat and a touch more water to the uncleaned brush.

12

Apply only in the lightest areas of the raccoon. Use the liner to brush-mix a watery beige with wheat and Whiteblend. Apply "scruffy" fur randomly in the light areas of the raccoon.

13

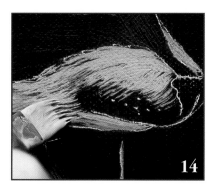

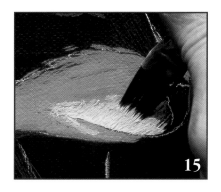

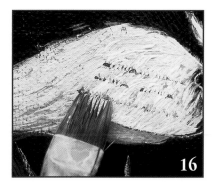

14 **Facial markings:** With the Multi-Texture brush, brush-mix a watery medium violet-gray. Apply medium violet-gray fur to the ears and facial markings. Create short, stubby muzzle fur by tapping the brush around. Vary the color and value occasionally by adding more Ultramarine Blue.

15 With the liner brush, apply Whiteblend around the mouth corner and along the bottom edge of the upper lip. Blend the Whiteblend around the mouth by patting with the Multi-Texture brush. Dry.

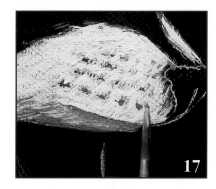

16 Use the Multi-Texture and liner brushes with Whiteblend to highlight the muzzle and facial markings. Tap the brush to highlight the short fur and drag it to highlight longer fur. Dry. Tap Titanium White highlights along the foremost areas of the facial markings and on the muzzle.

17 Darken the medium violet-gray with more Grumbacher Gray. Use this paint on the liner brush to emphasize the whisker indentations along the muzzle.

18 Brush-mix Burnt Sienna with a touch of Whiteblend to a milky consistency. Use the liner brush to highlight the side of the face and the bridge of his nose. While this is still wet, fade around the side of the face with the Multi-Texture brush moistened with Clearblend.

19 Use watery Whiteblend on the liner brush to apply the whiskers. Use a flat detail brush to apply a warm gray reflected light along the outer edges of the nose. With a small filbert brush moistened with Clearblend, soften the inside edges of the reflected light paint, creating a rounded appearance. To create a wet appearance, dab Whiteblend along the top bend of the nose.

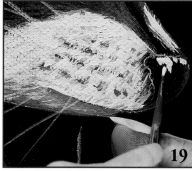

20 Use the liner to paint the feet charcoal. Highlight with warm gray. Use the liner with watery fur colors to pull a few fur strokes over the leg. With watery Mars Black on the liner brush, use C-strokes to make the claws. Apply the sunlit hay in front of the raccoon and falling out of the barn with various values of hay on the liner brush.

Sign and look to see if your "Bandit" is up to mischief! When the painting is thoroughly dry, remove excess graphite lines with a kneaded eraser or clean moist sponge. Spray your masterpiece with Grumbacher Acrylic Painting Varnish.

Handouts

Grumbacher Acrylic Colors

Burnt Sienna
Burnt Umber
Cadmium Yellow Medium
Grumbacher Red (Naphthol Red)
Thalo® Green (Blue Shade)
Thio™ Violet (Quinacridone Magenta)
Portrayt™ (Red Oxide)
Ultramarine Blue

Brushes

2" Gesso Brush
2" Hake Brush
#1 Bristle Fan Brush
Sable Essence™ ½" Angle Brush
Golden Edge™ #2 Liner Brush
Golden Edge™ #8 Filbert brush
Golden Edge™ #6 Flat Detail Brush

Other Supplies

14"x18" Stretched Canvas
Grumbacher Acrylic Painting Varnish
Whiteblend
Clearblend
Tapered Painting Knife
T-square Ruler
Black Graphite Paper
Stylus

Palette

Before you begin, prepare these color mixtures:

Pink—Whiteblend, touch of Grumbacher Red

Peach—Whiteblend, touch of Grumbacher Red, touch of Cadmium Yellow Medium

Sky Blue—3 parts Whiteblend, 1 part Ultramarine Blue, touch of Burnt Umber

Teal—3 parts Whiteblend, 1 part Ultramarine Blue, 1 part Thalo® Green

Aqua—1 part Thalo® Green, 1 part Ultramarine Blue, 1 part Whiteblend

Violet-Gray—3 parts Whiteblend, 1 part Ultramarine Blue, touch of Burnt Umber, touch of Thio™ Violet

Navy—5 parts Ultramarine Blue, 1 part Burnt Sienna

Blue-Gray—3 parts Whiteblend, 1 part Navy

Sand Gray—3 parts Whiteblend, 1 part Burnt Umber, 1 part Ultramarine Blue

1 **Canvas preparation:** Use the T-square to draw a horizon line 6" from the bottom of the canvas. Sketch the water and tide lines—don't transfer the boy or the birds yet. **Sky:** Use a wet-into-wet technique. Look at the finished painting for color placement. Use a gesso brush to cover the entire sky with Whiteblend. While it is wet, use the same brush to apply horizontal zig-zag streaks of pink, peach, sky blue, teal and violet-gray in the wet Whiteblend. While the colors are wet, blend as described in Step 2.

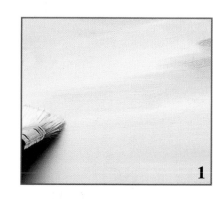

1

2 Use a clean towel-dried gesso brush to blend where the colors join. Do the final blending with the hake brush. Clean the brushes frequently with a paper towel during the blending process.

3 Apply and blend the water and sand colors horizontally. Begin painting across the horizon with the flat bristle brush loaded with violet-gray. Apply teal in the center and aqua behind the large wave in the center. Fill in the remaining water areas alternating among sky blue, teal and violet-gray.

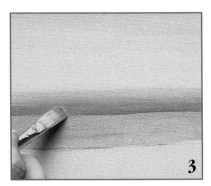

4 With a gesso brush, alternate peach and pink to cover the remaining canvas, overlapping the bottom of the water. Mix navy into the uncleaned brush, apply along the bottom of the canvas, and blend.

5 While the sand paint is wet, use the fan brush to randomly streak sand gray in the foreground and in the pink and peach areas. Add navy to the uncleaned brush and darken the tide lines at the water's edge. Blend with fan brush.

6 Use a touch of violet-gray to darken the foreground. Blend with a clean towel-dried fan or gesso brush. Dry thoroughly.

7 Transfer the boy, bucket, birds and tide lines.

8 Cover the water area with Clearblend and apply details while it is wet. Reapply the water colors if needed. To indicate whitecaps, use a liner brush or painting knife to apply horizontal dashes of Whiteblend in the distant water. Soften and fade the side and bottom edges with a filbert or flat bristle brush moistened with Clearblend. Fade the bottom edges of the tide lines into the sand.

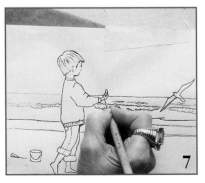

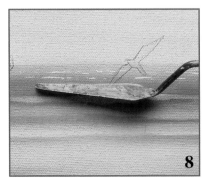

9 Use the fan brush with Whiteblend to stipple whitecaps along the top of the large breaker. Add a few spots of violet-gray in the bottom of the wet Whiteblend to shadow the rolling water. Be sure not to paint over the boy.

10 While it is still wet, use the filbert brush moistened with Clearblend in elongated C-strokes to pull down the bottom of the Whiteblend.

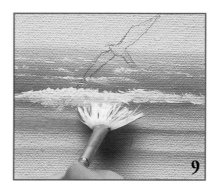

11 Holding the angle brush horizontally, load Whiteblend on the bottom and apply it along the foremost edge of the receding water nearest the large breaker. Fade out the ends.

12 While the Whiteblend is still wet, moisten a filbert brush with Clearblend and blend the top edge by stroking horizontally, zig-zagging gradually upward, allowing the paint to disappear at the bottom of the large breaker. Apply the next tide line and blend the top as before so that it disappears before it touches the previous tide line. Repeat, adding as many tide lines as you choose.

13 Load a flat detail brush with Clearblend and violet-gray to apply horizontal, translucent shadows under and to the left of the toys, boy's feet, and birds.

14 Use a detail or filbert brush to paint the bucket Cadmium Yellow Medium. Add Burnt Umber to the uncleaned brush and apply a shadow along the left side of the wet bucket. Blend. Paint Burnt Umber inside the bucket. Dry. With the liner brush, mix Cadmium Yellow Medium and Whiteblend, then apply the bucket rim and the handle. When these are dry, add watery Burnt Umber shadows under them. With the liner and Grumbacher Red, paint a shovel near the bucket.

15 Apply and blend one area of flesh at a time. Use the filbert with a mixture of Portrayt™ and Whiteblend; while it is wet, shadow it with the liner, using brush-mixed Portrayt™ and a touch of Ultramarine Blue. Blend with a clean, towel-dried liner or filbert brush.

16 Paint the boy's hair with the filbert brush and creamy Burnt Umber (or the color of your choice). After the hair is dry, brush-mix Burnt Umber and peach to streak tan highlights on his hair.

17 Use the liner brush with Cadmium Yellow Medium to paint the collar and cuff of his undershirt. Add Whiteblend to the uncleaned brush for highlights. Use the angle brush with navy to paint his sweatshirt.

18 Add Whiteblend to the uncleaned brush to highlight the wet shirt. Add finishing highlights of teal. Blend with a clean towel-dried brush. Dry. Touch up if needed with the appropriate color. Use Clearblend on a clean moist brush to blend away unwanted hard edges. Load the liner with navy to add the waistband around the sweatshirt bottom. Highlight with teal and light blue. Dry.

19 Use the angle or flat detail brush with Whiteblend to paint the pants. Shadow with blue-gray; blend while they are still wet. Dry, then add details with the liner brush. Soften unwanted hard edges with a Clearblend-moistened brush.

20 Moisten the sand with Clearblend. Use an angle brush loaded with Whiteblend to create water marks on the sand. Blend the top edges away from the line by stroking horizontally, moving the paint gradually upward.

21 Use the liner and filbert brushes to paint and blend one large seagull at a time. Apply violet-gray first and add Whiteblend highlights while the dark is still wet. Blend with a clean towel-dried brush. Use brush-mixed Grumbacher Red and Cadmium Yellow Medium to paint their feet and beaks. Dry. Use a watery mixture of navy and Burnt Umber to paint the eyes and primary feathers. Follow step 11 to apply shadows to the left of the walking gulls' feet.

22 Use a liner double loaded with violet-gray and Whiteblend to make the small flying gulls.

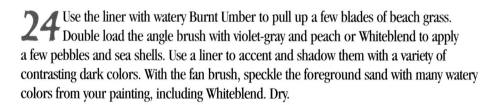

23 Moisten the sand under the large flying gull with Clearblend. While it is wet, use the liner with violet-gray to add a translucent shadow. Blot the shadow if it appears too opaque.

24 Use the liner with watery Burnt Umber to pull up a few blades of beach grass. Double load the angle brush with violet-gray and peach or Whiteblend to apply a few pebbles and sea shells. Use a liner to accent and shadow them with a variety of contrasting dark colors. With the fan brush, speckle the foreground sand with many watery colors from your painting, including Whiteblend. Dry.

Sign your painting and go feed the birds! Use a kneaded eraser or a clean moist sponge to remove any excess graphite marks. Spray your thoroughly dry painting with Grumbacher Acrylic Painting Varnish.

Marsh Landing

Grumbacher Acrylic Colors
Burnt Umber
Cadmium Yellow Medium
Mars Black
Prussian Blue
Sap Green
Titanium White
Ultramarine Blue
Yellow Ochre Light

Brushes
2" Gesso Brush
Golden Edge™ #8 Filbert Brush
Sable Essence™ ½" Angle Brush
Golden Edge™ #6 Round Brush
Golden Edge™ #2 Liner Brush
Multi-Texture Brush

Other Supplies
16"x20" Stretched Canvas
Matte Medium & Varnish
Clearblend
Whiteblend
Rapidograph Technical Pen #2.00
Rotring Artist Brown Ink
Masking Tape
16"x20" Mat Template (11½"x15½" Opening)
White graphite paper
Tapered Painting Knife
stylus, Natural Sponge

Palette
Before you begin, prepare these color mixtures:

Hunter Green—1 part Prussian Blue, 1 part Sap Green (mix about 2 tablespoons, add water and stir to the consistency of Whiteblend)

Bright Yellow—8 parts Titanium White, 1 part Cadmium Yellow Medium, Water

Teal—10 parts Whiteblend, 1 part Prussian Blue

Sky Blue—10 parts Whiteblend, 1 part Ultramarine Blue

Leaf Green—2 parts Hunter Green, 2 parts Whiteblend, 1 part Cadmium Yellow Medium

Yellow-Green—2 parts Whiteblend, 1 part Leaf Green, 1 part Cadmium Yellow Medium

Off-White—Titanium White, tiny touch of Cadmium Yellow Medium

1 **Canvas preparation:** Place the canvas on a flat surface. Align the edges of the mat template on the canvas and use the pen to draw a line along the inner edge of the opening. Hold the mat securely in place as you slowly pull the pen along the edges. Repeat if you would like a bolder mark. Dry. Remove the template and cover the border with masking tape so it extends ½" inside the marked line. Press the tape down tightly. Use a fan or gesso brush to seal the inner edges of the tape with Matte Medium. Blend the inside edge of the medium toward the center of the canvas, leaving no abrupt ridge along the edge of the paint. Dry. With a very moist gesso brush, quickly cover the canvas inside the tape with a generous amount of hunter green.

2 With a clean, moist sponge, pat and blot the canvas to remove paint from the center area, creating the illusion of light filtering through dense foliage. Repeat to remove more color. After the desired amount of paint is removed in the center, lightly tap around the remaining areas to create texture, but remove less paint. Dry. Transfer the bird, placing the center of its eye 7½" from the top of the canvas and 6¼" from the right side.

3 Use a liner brush with Yellow Ochre Light to paint the eye and beak. While this is wet, highlight the bottom of the eye and the top of the beak with creamy bright yellow. Dry. Use the liner loaded with watery Burnt Umber to draw curved lines (like parentheses) on both sides of the eye, then to paint a nostril, markings between the eye and beak, and a thin line separating the upper and lower beak. Use Mars Black to paint a round pupil in the eye center. Dry. Load a clean liner brush with Whiteblend and place a catchlight at 11:00.

4 Alternate using the filbert, angle and liner brushes to basecoat the body—apply and blend one section at a time. Use teal as the base color; create three values of teal by adding more and more Whiteblend to the brush to progressively lighten it. Apply the lightest values on the bottom wing feathers, legs and belly. Apply the middle value in the center of the wing area and the base color in the remaining areas. Add a touch of hunter green to the wet teal as you apply paint in the most shadowed areas under the wings and tail.

5 While each area is wet, blend with a clean, towel-dried angle brush. Lightly brush back and forth in the direction of the feather growth. Dry.

6 Highlight one section at a time. Apply Clearblend over the bottom half of the head and the right half of the neck. While the Clearblend is wet, use the liner brush to apply Whiteblend on the top of the head and the left side of the neck. Stroke the brush in the direction of the feather growth, allowing the tips of some feathers to separate along the bend from the head to the neck. Blend the inside edges of the Whiteblend around the head and neck with a small filbert brush moistened with Clearblend.

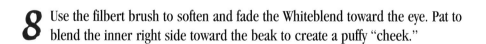

7 Use a liner brush to apply a curved line of Whiteblend along the side of the head in the ear area.

8 Use the filbert brush to soften and fade the Whiteblend toward the eye. Pat to blend the inner right side toward the beak to create a puffy "cheek."

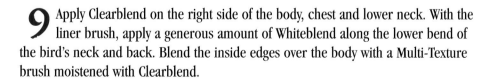

9 Apply Clearblend on the right side of the body, chest and lower neck. With the liner brush, apply a generous amount of Whiteblend along the lower bend of the bird's neck and back. Blend the inside edges over the body with a Multi-Texture brush moistened with Clearblend.

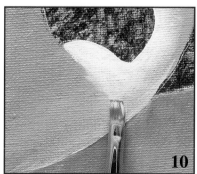

10 Add a touch of teal to the Whiteblend in the liner and apply a reflected light along the right edge of the bird's body and lower neck. Blend the inside edge of the reflected light into the body and neck with a Multi-Texture brush moistened with Clearblend.

11 Mix Whiteblend and Clearblend with the Multi-Texture brush and indicate a hint of light hitting the bottom edges of the feather rows under the wings. Use light strokes to add a few additional feather strokes on the body.

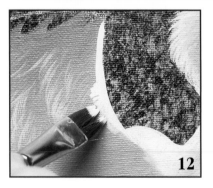

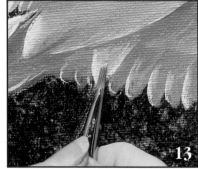

12 Use the liner brush to apply Whiteblend along the top of the bird's wings. Moisten the Multi-Texture brush with Clearblend; soften the lower edges of this section, making the bottom ragged and creating the illusion of light hitting tiny feathers along the leading edge of the wing.

13 Highlight the most sunlit areas with off-white. Work one area at a time. Apply the off-white with the small round brush; blend the inside edges of the wet highlight paint with a Multi-Texture brush moistened with Clearblend. Apply and blend the highlights on the top of the head, the top of the back, top of the tail, and the left sides of the thighs.

14 Use the liner brush to apply an off-white highlight on the leading edges of the primary feathers along the bottoms of the wings. Blend the inside edge of the wet highlight paint by stroking the Multi-Texture brush in the direction of the barbs on the primary feathers, away from the light.

15 Double load the liner brush with Mars Black and sky blue to paint the legs. Use an angle brush to remove or straighten unwanted crooks or bulges on the legs—or wipe them off completely with a clean moist sponge, dry and reapply. Touch up light and dark irregularities after they are dry.

16 Use the liner brush with a brush mixture of hunter green and Whiteblend to paint the ferns and foliage around the bird's feet. Blot the bases of the ferns with your finger to "plant" them. Add leaf green to the uncleaned brush to highlight a few fronds of some ferns and to add a few brighter clumps.

17 Add yellow-green to the brush and highlight some leaves on a few clumps. Vary each value to create a range of colors. Dry.

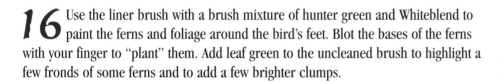

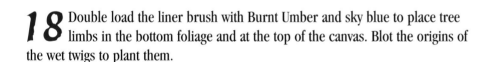

18 Double load the liner brush with Burnt Umber and sky blue to place tree limbs in the bottom foliage and at the top of the canvas. Blot the origins of the wet twigs to plant them.

19 Apply leaves on the twigs at the top of the canvas with the same colors as you used for the foliage below the bird. Dry thoroughly.

Sign your painting. Use a kneaded eraser or a clean moist sponge to remove the excess transfer marks. Remove the masking tape by lifting and pulling it toward the center of the canvas; use Whiteblend to touch up around the border if needed. Spray the finished painting with Grumbacher Acrylic Painting Varnish. Enjoy the majesty of your "marsh landing."

A Walk in the Park

Grumbacher Acrylic Colors
Burnt Umber
Cadmium Red Light
Cadmium Yellow Medium
Green Gold
Grumbacher Payne's Gray
Grumbacher Purple (Dioxazine Purple)
Grumbacher Red (Naphthol Red)
Hooker's Green
Thalo® Crimson
Titanium White
Ultramarine Blue

Brushes
2" Gesso Brush
2" Hake Brush
Gainsborough® #6 Flat Bristle Brush
Eterna #6 Round Bristle Brush
Golden Edge™ #8 Filbert Brush
Golden Edge™ #2 Liner Bbrush
#1 Bristle Fan Brush
Sable Essence™ ½" Angle Brush

Other Supplies
16"x20" Stretched Canvas
Matte Medium & Varnish
Clearblend
Whiteblend
Tapered Painting Knife
Natural Sponge
Graphite Paper: Black, White
16"x20" Mat Template (11½"x15½" Opening)
Rapidograph Technical Pen #2.00
Rotring Artist Ink: Brown
Masking Tape, Stylus

Palette
Before you begin, prepare these color mixtures:

Pale Peach—Whiteblend, touch of Monoazo Orange, touch of Cadmium Yellow Medium

Medium Violet-Gray—6 parts Whiteblend, 4 parts Ultramarine Blue, 4 parts Grumbacher Gray, 1 part Thalo® Crimson

Light Violet-Gray—1 part Whiteblend, 1 part Medium Violet-Gray

Off-White—4 parts Whiteblend, 1 part Pale Peach, 1 part Light Violet-Gray (mix about two tablespoons)

Dark Green—3 parts Grumbacher Gray, 1 part Hooker's Green

Light Pastel Gray-Green—4 parts Light Violet-Gray, 1 part Dark Green

Yellow-Green—3 parts Green Gold, 2 parts Whiteblend, 1 part Cadmium Yellow Medium

1 **Canvas preparation:** Paint the canvas off-white. Dry; if the color appears uneven, reapply. Place the dry canvas face up on a flat surface. Align the mat template with the canvas edges and use the pen to draw a line along the inner edge of the opening. Hold the mat securely in place as you slowly pull the pen along the edges. Repeat if you want a bolder mark. Dry. Remove the template and cover the border with masking tape. Position the tape so it extends ³⁄₈" inside the drawn lines. Press it down tightly. Use a fan or gesso brush to seal the inner edges with Matte Medium. Blend the inside edges toward the center, leaving no abrupt ridges. Transfer the steps and the shapes of the surrounding bushes with black graphite paper, placing the bottom step just above the edge of the tape. (The fence and trellis will be transferred after the foliage is dry.) Use the flat bristle brush to paint the front edges of the steps Grumbacher Gray. Paint the tops of the steps and the path medium violet-gray. Dry.

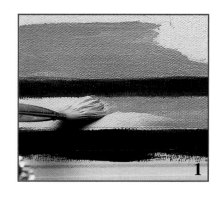

2 Background: Use the gesso brush to cover the top ⅓ of the sky pale peach. Wipe excess paint from the brush and apply the shapes of the distant trees with light violet-gray. Blend with a light, erratic stroke of the dry hake brush to create a misty, out-of-focus appearance.

3 Foliage: While the background is still wet, use the sponge to mix and apply the remaining foliage. Make each value slightly darker as you move downward by adding darker colors to the uncleaned sponge. Load a mixture of light violet-gray and violet-gray on the sponge and tap it around in the lower areas of the wet light violet-gray foliage. Blend as before; clean the hake brush often as you blend.

4 Add light pastel gray-green to the uncleaned sponge and apply a lower area of foliage that overlaps the lower portion of the distant foliage. Sponge-mix a slightly darker value by adding a touch more dark green to the uncleaned sponge. Repeat, painting the foliage darker each time as you paint lower on the canvas. Do not mist out the medium and dark foliage. To fill in the darkest areas of the foliage quickly, pile the paint in these areas with the painting knife.

5 Move the paint around by tapping over it with the uncleaned sponge. Use a sponge to connect the distant and foreground foliage by tapping a few tall dark trees over the distant foliage on both sides of the canvas and behind where the arbor will go.

6 To connect the walkway and foliage, work with dark green on the sponge and medium violet-gray on the flat bristle brush. Use the sponge to create a section of foliage overlapping the edge of the walkway or step. Stroke the flat bristle brush horizontally over the bottom of the wet dark green paint, blending it with the medium violet-gray to create shadows on the walkway.

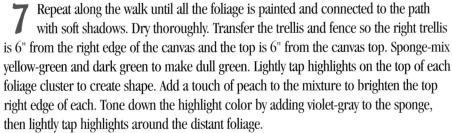

7 Repeat along the walk until all the foliage is painted and connected to the path with soft shadows. Dry thoroughly. Transfer the trellis and fence so the right trellis is 6" from the right edge of the canvas and the top is 6" from the canvas top. Sponge-mix yellow-green and dark green to make dull green. Lightly tap highlights on the top of each foliage cluster to create shape. Add a touch of peach to the mixture to brighten the top right edge of each. Tone down the highlight color by adding violet-gray to the sponge, then lightly tap highlights around the distant foliage.

8 **Fence:** With the liner, brush-mix light violet-gray with a touch of Ultramarine Blue and Whiteblend. Double load this gray-blue with Whiteblend to paint the fence posts. Blot the bottoms to "plant" them in the dark foliage. For the small posts, use less paint and less pressure on the brush. Add a ball to the top of each large post. Dry, then highlight the top left edges with Whiteblend and blend the inner edges to round them.

9 **Trellis:** Use the liner to paint the far side gray-blue; if needed, adjust the color for contrast. Double load the liner with gray-blue and Whiteblend for the near side. Dry. Use Whiteblend to highlight a few edges on the far side.

10 **Flowers:** Apply with a clean sponge. Lightly tap to apply brush-mixed Thalo® Crimson and a touch of Grumbacher Purple for the shadow of the pink azaleas. Add Thalo® Crimson and Whiteblend to the uncleaned sponge for the azalea blooms. Place the bloom on the top left ⅔ of the bush. Use the same colors to create a flowering tree right of the trellis, but use upwardly-thrusting strokes of the sponge for a different look. Lightly tap a hint of these colors in a few other places in the foreground.

11 With a clean sponge and the gray-blue mixture from step 10, apply the shadow color for the white gardenia at the left center. Add Whiteblend to the sponge and highlight the top left ⅔ of the bush. Use a darker or different value of any gray for the shadow of the right front white bush. Highlight the top left ⅔ of the bush with Whiteblend.

12 Using a clean sponge and a mixture of Cadmium Yellow Medium and Grumbacher Purple, apply the shadows for all the orange and yellow bushes. Sponge-mix Cadmium Yellow Medium and Whiteblend to highlight the top left ⅔ of the yellow bushes in front of the trellis. Add a touch of Titanium White to the uncleaned sponge and add a brighter highlight on the top left ⅓ of these bushes.

13 Wipe excess paint off the sponge, add Monoazo Orange and apply orange blooms to the bush on the far left. Add Whiteblend and Monoazo Orange to the uncleaned sponge and lightly tap highlights as before. Add Titanium White and Monoazo Orange to a clean spot on the sponge and apply sparser highlights.

14 For the remainder of the foreground flowers, create a mixture of colors of your choice from the garden. Do not make these as bright as the others. Dry.

15 Use the liner brush and watery dark green to paint a vine growing on the trellis. Skip spots, making it appear to grow in front of and behind the braces. Highlight with watery yellow-green. Use the filbert brush to add a few dark green and yellow-green leaves.

16 **Roses:** Use the liner brush to apply squiggly dots of brush-mixed colors. Use marbleized Grumbacher Red and Whiteblend for some; for others, use various marbleized values of Grumbacher Red and Titanium White.

17 **Walk and steps:** With a flat bristle brush, cover the steps and walkway with Clearblend. Use the same brush to stroke translucent violet-gray over the front edges to lighten the dark. While the Clearblend is wet, apply horizontal dashes of any flower highlight color in the central area of the walkway to brighten it, being careful to avoid the shadow areas. Add touches of peach along the leading edge of each section nearest the front edges to indicate dappled sunlight filtering through the trees. Dry.

18 With a clean flat bristle brush, apply Clearblend over the upright front edges. Alternate using the flat bristle, angle, and filbert brushes to create oddly shaped stones in the wet Clearblend. Use lighter, contrasting values of gray and pink from the painting for the stones. Make quick irregular strokes; do not paint the stones solidly. Should they become too solid, smudge areas of the wet stones with your finger.

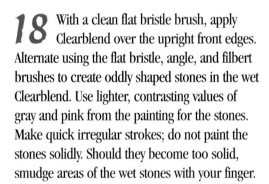

19 **Details:** Double load the liner brush with violet-gray and peach to add a few tree trunks.

20 Use the fan brush turned vertically and the azalea colors to stipple hollyhocks in the right foreground. With a round bristle brush, Titanium White and a touch of Thalo® Crimson, tap brighter pink highlights blooms on the blooms. Use a clean round bristle brush with Titanium White to highlight the gardenias. With a mixture of the azalea highlight colors and violet-gray, tap lightly to apply a sprinkle of "toned down" flowers in the distant foliage.

21 Use the filbert brush with Titanium White and the flower colors to apply petals on some of the foreground flowers, brush-mixing various values.

Sign your painting. Dry, then remove the tape by lifting it and pulling toward the center of the canvas. Touch up any seepage with off-white. Take a leisurely walk in the park and smell the flowers! When the painting is thoroughly dry, use a kneaded eraser or damp sponge to remove any excess pencil lines. Spray with Grumbacher Acrylic Picture Varnish.

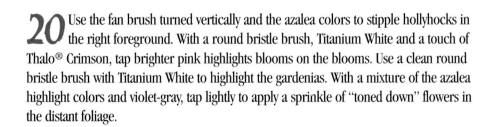

Rolling In

Grumbacher Acrylic Colors
Burnt Sienna
Burnt Umber
Cadmium Yellow Medium
Grumbacher Payne's Gray
Grumbacher Purple (Dioxazine Purple)
Monoazo Orange
Portrayt™ (Red Oxide)
Sap Green
Titanium White
Ultramarine Blue

Brushes
Two #1 Bristle Fan Brushes
2" Hake Brush
Two 2" Gesso Brushes
Golden Edge™ #6 Flat Brush
Multi-Texture Brush
Golden Edge™ #2 Liner Brush
Sable Essence™ ½" Angle Brush

Other Supplies
16"x20" Stretched Canvas
Grumbacher Acrylic Painting Varnish
Grumbacher Acrylic Retarder
Whiteblend
Clearblend
Tapered Painting Knife
Natural Sponge
White Graphite Paper, Stylus
Adhesive Design Protector

Palette

Before you begin, prepare these color mixtures:

Navy—2 parts Grumbacher Gray, 1 part Ultramarine Blue
(Mix 1 Tablespoon)

Blue-Gray—20 parts Whiteblend, 2 parts Grumbacher Gray,
1 part Ultramarine Blue

Medium Blue—4 parts Navy, 1 part Whiteblend, touch of
Grumbacher Purple

Pale Peach—1 part Whiteblend, 1 part Titanium White,
tiny touch of Monoazo Orange

Dark Blue-Green—2 parts Ultramarine Blue, 1 part Sap Green

Gray-Green—2 parts Medium Blue, 2 parts Dark Blue-Green,
1 part Whiteblend

Sunny Yellow—Whiteblend, touch of Cadmium Yellow Medium

Light Violet-Gray—3 parts Whiteblend, 1 part Navy,
touch of Grumbacher Purple

Pale Blue—6 parts Whiteblend, 1 part Ultramarine Blue

1 **Canvas preparation:** Position the canvas vertically and use a gesso brush to paint it Grumbacher Gray. While it is wet, add Whiteblend to the uncleaned brush and paint a horizontal streak through the center of the wet paint, creating a medium blue-gray area. Blend by stroking a clean, towel-dried gesso brush horizontally; dry. Transfer the design with white graphite paper so the front peak of the barn roof is 8" from the right side of the canvas and 8¾" from the bottom. Transfer the barn and silo to a design protector. Cut out, align it carefully and adhere it tightly over the barn and silo. **Sky:** Apply retarder to the sky area. Work the sky wet into wet.

1

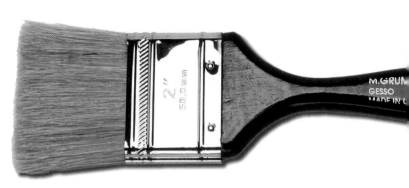

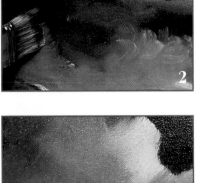

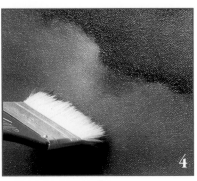

2 Reapply retarder or Clearblend to soften or blend hard edges as needed, working one part of the sky at a time. Load a gesso brush with navy and cover the top ⅓ of the sky, occasionally adding medium blue. Continue adding the navy and medium blue, but not solidly—apply the color with small circular scrubbing motions, creating cloud-like drifts of dark coming across the sky behind the silo and barn, also from the right side of the canvas. Leave open areas above right of the barn and along the horizon.

3 Continue while the navy, medium blue and retarder are still wet. Wipe any excess dark paint from the brush and pick up pale blue. Use the same circular strokes to apply clouds in the top section, then apply blue-gray along the bottoms of the dark clouds in the center and bottom of the sky.

4 Blend, first with a clean towel-dried gesso brush, then with the hake. Use a gentle touch and an erratic motion. Continue while the painting is wet. Touch up hard or rough edges with the fan brush. If the paint will not blend, moisten the fan brush with Clearblend.

5 Moisten the lower sky again with retarder. Paint it with lighter values of the sky colors, making smaller clouds and streaks. While it is wet, zigzag streaks of pale peach through the bottom section of the sky with the fan brush. With the same brush, add streaks of blue-gray, varying the value by occasionally brush mixing in navy or medium blue. Leave this lower sky streaky. Apply pale peach above and behind the top of the barn roof with circular strokes of the fan brush. Lessen the pressure on the brush at the edges, creating a gradual transition of color.

6 Blend the lower portion of the sky with the gesso brush, stroking horizontally back and forth. Use short, erratic strokes of a hake brush to soften the brush marks and edges. Clean the blending brush frequently.

7 Complete the final blending with the fan brush. Add Clearblend or additional color as needed. When blending or applying color, use more pressure to apply or loosen the paint, then gradually lessen the pressure until you are using a very light touch. Dry thoroughly.

8 **Foliage and grass:** Use the fan brush to tap gray-green trees along the horizon left of the barn. Apply gray-green and blue-gray trees on the right. Create depth in the meadows by painting light values (blue-gray and gray-green) in the distance, dark values (blue-black, navy and dark blue-green) in the foreground, and a mixture of these colors in the middle section. Create and blend one meadow at a time, starting with the most distant meadow, then proceed, making the colors slightly darker each time.

9 Apply the blue-gray and blue-green base paint to the meadow with the fan brush. While it is still wet, remove any excess paint from the fan brush and lightly load the tips of the bristles with sunny yellow. Holding the brush almost flat against the canvas, with the handle down and the bristles pointing up, hit the brush against the canvas along the crest of the meadow. Clean the brush, hold it vertically and tap around in the lower portion of the highlight paint to blend, creating a gradual transition of color. Repeat for the distant meadows. Repeat the process for the middle meadow, applying a medium-value base coat as described in step 8.

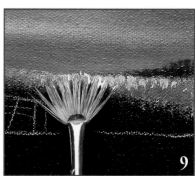

10 Use the gesso brush to apply dark blue-green, navy and medium blue base paint in the foreground. Apply gray-green and blue-gray along the crest of the front meadow. Add blue-gray and gray-green to the uncleaned gesso brush, then create texture with the gesso brush by tapping and crunching into the wet dark paint. Hold the brush so that the handle is perpendicular to the canvas and crunch it lightly in the distant meadow, harder in the lower sections. Apply sunny yellow highlights along the meadow ridges and blend the outer edges with the fan as before, leaving the central areas unblended. Dry thoroughly. Remove the design protector.

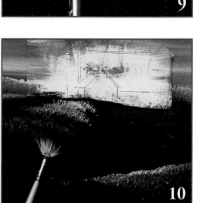

11 **Silo:** With the angle brush, use the sky colors to mix a contrasting medium gray; paint the dome of the silo. Use the liner to add pale blue to the top right side of the dome and blend while wet with a clean angle brush. After the dome is dry, use the liner with pale blue to add the curved, pie-shaped ridges on top.

12 Use the angle brush with light violet-gray to paint the bottom, center and left side of the silo base (the area shown in shadow in the larger photo at the top right). With a clean angle brush loaded with Whiteblend and a touch of pale peach, paint the top right side. Blend by brushing up and down, overlapping the wet violet-gray. Use the liner to add a thin line of Whiteblend reflected light along the left edge; blend with a clean dry angle brush. Use Clearblend to soften the edges if the paint won't blend. Dry. With the liner brush and watery Grumbacher Gray, apply a thin, curved shadow under the dome.

13 **Barn:** Use the angle brush with Whiteblend and pale peach to paint the top of the barn roof. Paint the bottom with light violet-gray. Blend with a clean, dry angle brush; stroke the brush following the angle of the roof.

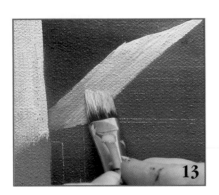

14 Use the angle brush to paint the left side of the barn Burnt Umber and the front Burnt Sienna. Lightly streak Portrayt™ over the wet paint with a Multi-Texture brush. Add a touch of Whiteblend to the uncleaned brush and add lighter streaks on the front. With a clean Multi-Texture brush, apply streaks of blue-gray on both sides.

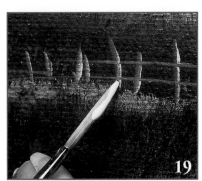

15 **Outbuilding and foundation:** With the angle brush, paint and blend one section at a time. Paint the bottom of the roof Grumbacher Gray and the top blue-gray; blend. Alternate between light violet-gray and Whiteblend to paint the base of the barn and the sides of the outbuilding. Dry.

16 **Details:** Use the flat detail brush to paint the barn window, door and roof with watery Grumbacher Gray. Add a touch of blue-gray for the outbuilding. Add the moldings with a clean liner brush and Whiteblend. Dry. Paint the molding shadows with a liner brush loaded with watery Grumbacher Gray.

17 Add "do-fors" (things that are determined by the viewer's imagination that we "do," "for" the scene is too sterile and perfect without them). Use a variety of colors and brushes from the painting. Paint the barrel Burnt Sienna and Whiteblend, shadowed with Burnt Umber.

18 Brush-mix peach, sunny yellow and Whiteblend to make off-white; use the angle brush to paint the trailer. Shadow with Burnt Umber. When the trailer is dry, use the liner with watery Burnt Umber to add a wheel and tongue; highlight with off-white.

19 Double load the liner with violet-gray and Whiteblend to paint the fences. If you choose, add tiny birds.

Sign, and take cover before the storm comes rolling in! Touch up as needed. When the painting is thoroughly dry, remove any excess graphite lines with a kneaded eraser or damp sponge. Spray with Grumbacher Acrylic Painting Varnish.

Tropical Breeze

Grumbacher Acrylic Colors
Burnt Umber
Cadmium Yellow Medium
Green Gold
Grumbacher Purple (Dioxazine Purple)
Grumbacher Red (Naphthol Red)
Prussian Blue
Sap Green
Thalo® Blue
Ultramarine Blue

Brushes
2" Gesso Brush
2" Hake Brush
#1 Bristle Fan Brush
Golden Edge™ #2 Liner Brush
Sable Essence™ ½" Angle Brush
Gainsborough® #6 Flat Bristle Brush
Professional #6 Bristle Filbert Brush

Other Supplies
16"x20" Stretched Canvas
Grumbacher Acrylic Painting Varnish
Grumbacher Modeling Paste
Whiteblend
Clearblend
Grumbacher Retarder
Tapered Painting Knife
Natural Sponge
Plastic Fork
Black Graphite Paper, Stylus

Palette
Before you begin painting (the second day), prepare these colors:

Medium Teal—30 parts Whiteblend, 3 parts Thalo® Blue, 1 part Ultramarine Blue

Violet-Gray—16 parts Whiteblend, 8 parts Ultramarine Blue, 1 part Burnt Umber, 1 part Grumbacher Purple

Pink—Whiteblend, touch of Grumbacher Red

Pale Yellow—Whiteblend, touch of Cadmium Yellow Medium

Marbleized Peach—Pink, Pale Yellow

Pale Blue—20 parts Whiteblend, 1 part Thalo® Blue

Seafoam—Pale Blue, Pale Yellow

Medium Blue—2 parts Violet-Gray, 1 part Prussian Blue

Dark Green—1 part Prussian Blue, 1 part Sap Green

Terra Cotta—2 parts Cadmium Yellow Medium, 1 part Grumbacher Red, 20 parts Whiteblend

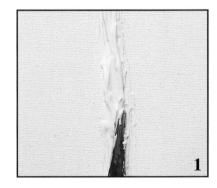

1

1 **Canvas preparation:** A day in advance of painting, transfer and sketch the design so that the waterline is 5½" from the canvas bottom, the distant hill is 1½" tall, the sand dune at the bottom is 1½" from the bottom of the canvas with the tallest grass 3" high, the small palm is 11" tall, and the large palm extends off the top right corner. Using the sketch and the finished painting as a guide, sculpt the hills, water, tide lines, sand and tree trunks with the painting knife and modeling paste, leaving clumps and ridges of texture on the designs.

2 **Grass and palm fronds:** Apply the paste with the knife, then scrape through it with a plastic fork to create individual fronds and grass blades. To create rough texture, pat the wet paste with the painting knife or fork. Dry overnight.

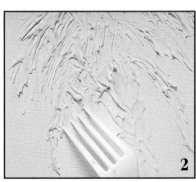

2

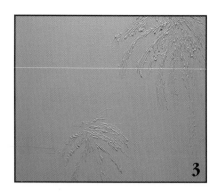

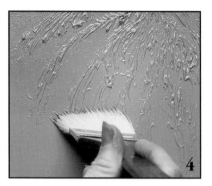

3 Paint the dry, sculpted canvas medium teal. Dry thoroughly. Mix the remaining colors when you are ready to paint.

4 **Sky:** Use a gesso brush loaded with Grumbacher Retarder and cover the top half of the sky. Clean the excess from the brush and load it with violet-gray. Apply a cloud formation along the top of the wet sky. Blend with the hake brush to create a blustery, translucent drifting cloud.

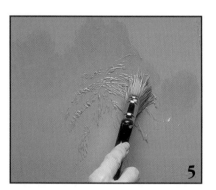

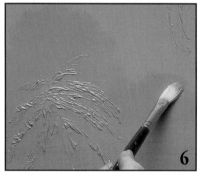

5 Cover the remainder of the sky with Grumbacher Retarder. While it is wet, use the corner of the gesso brush to apply billowing violet-gray cloud shapes through the center of the sky. Apply the tops of the clouds with an erratic, circular stroke.

6 At the bottom of the cloud formation, stroke the brush horizontally to create a somewhat flat bottom and drifts of color in the sky. Add streaks of medium teal throughout the bottom and below the cloud; blend. Use the filbert brush to blend and create a bumpy top edge on the billowing clouds. Soften and blend with the hake brush as needed. Tap around the edges with the brush to define the cloud's shape.

7 Use a fan brush to apply peach at the bottom of the sky along the horizon. Clean the brush, then moisten it with Clearblend and gradually blend the peach up into the sky by brushing horizontally back and forth. Dry.

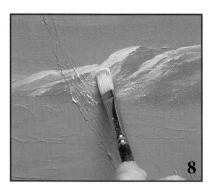

8 **Distant hills:** Use the flat brush to scumble violet-gray over the textured distant hills. Do not brush until it is smooth and solid. Clean the flat brush, load it with peach, and highlight the top and left sides of the hill formations, allowing the peach to grab on the textured ridges.

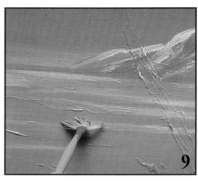

9

9 **Water:** Work the water wet-into-wet. Cover the water area with retarder and reapply as often as needed. Add colors to the water area and blend while the Retarder is wet, but do not paint it solid; leave some of the basecoat showing. Using the large photo as a guide, use the fan brush to apply horizontal streaks of pale blue, seafoam, and violet-gray in the water area. Blend with the gesso brush, fading at the sides of the canvas.

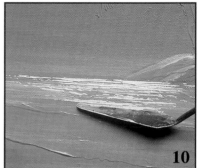

10

10 While the water is still wet, use the painting knife to apply horizontal streaks of Whiteblend in the distant water. Blend with a fan brush to create bright shimmery areas left of the short palm tree and randomly throughout the distant water. Fade the ends and below each streak to "plant" them in the water. Add teal streaks to the right of the Whiteblend.

11

11 Use elongated backwards C-strokes of the fan brush to create the large wave. Apply medium blue, then seafoam. Do not blend; leave light and dark streaks.

12 With the fan brush, crunch Whiteblend foam along the crest of the large wave, tapering at the ends. Use a clean brush moistened with Clearblend to pull down the bottom of some Whiteblend with the same backwards C-strokes. Do not overblend; leave streaks.

12

13 Use the angle brush to alternately apply medium blue and violet-gray shadows under the tide lines. Blend the bottom edges of the wet shadow paint by stroking horizontally, gradually moving downward. Use the angle brush to apply pink and white to the raised leading edges. Blend the top edge with a clean fan brush moistened with Clearblend, brushing horizontally and gradually moving upward. Apply pale yellow between the foremost tide line and the dune. Blend with a flat brush moistened with Clearblend. Dry. Re-wet the water area with Clearblend and add more dark or light as needed. Blend unwanted hard edges away with a brush moistened with Clearblend. Dry.

13

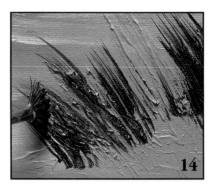

14 Use the fan brush loaded with watery dark green to lift up the grasses around the bases of the trees.

15 Pat lightly with the sponge loaded with dark green to create the foliage.

16 With the flat brush, apply Burnt Umber to the dune, attaching it to the grass. With a clean flat brush, streak terra cotta highlights across the dune; do not overblend. Dry.

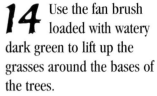

17 Load a filbert brush with Clearblend and lightly wipe excess on a paper towel. Cover the upper sky area and upper clouds with Clearblend. Alternate loading peach, pink and Whiteblend on the fan brush to apply dashes of each color along the bottoms of the wet overhead clouds. Blend the colors up into the clouds with the filbert brush moistened with Clearblend.

18 Highlight and blend one puff of the billowing middle clouds at a time. Use the fan brush to apply dabbles of marbleized peach on the top left edge of a cloud. Use a filbert brush moistened with Clearblend to pat-blend the bottom and inner edges of this highlight. Stagger the pats and skip spaces between pats to create rolling, billowing, puffy clouds. Pat around on the cloud until the highlight color gradually disappears. Apply more highlight and repeat. Clean and reload the filbert brush often. Load the filbert brush with more Clearblend and a touch of the cloud highlight colors. Streak across the bottom of the sky under the middle cloud. Blend.

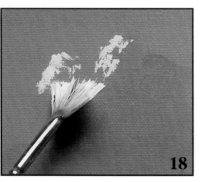

19 **Foreground:** Use the flat brush and Burnt Umber to make the tree trunks. Highlight the left sides of the trunks with terra cotta and blend into the centers. Use a liner brush to apply a thin, broken pale blue line of reflected light on the right edges.

20 Load the fan brush with dark green and paint the palm fronds. To avoid blobs, mix water with dark green to a consistency thinner than Whiteblend.

21 Mix Green Gold into the uncleaned brush and streak highlights on some left and center fronds. Mix in more Green Gold and some pale yellow and sparingly streak this light yellow green highlight on sunny spots.

22 Use the sponge to dabble the same highlights onto the grass. Add red and a touch of pale yellow for accents.

23 Double load the angle brush with Burnt Umber and terra cotta to make the coconuts on the sand.

24 Use a liner brush double loaded with violet-gray and Whiteblend to paint the birds. Brush-mix watery Burnt Umber and Ultramarine Blue, then use the liner to paint the wing tips and eyes. With the liner, mix Grumbacher Red, Cadmium Yellow Medium and a touch of Whiteblend to paint their beaks orange.

Sign your painting and bask in your "tropical breeze!" When thoroughly dry, use a kneaded eraser or moist sponge to remove any excess graphite lines. Spray with Grumbacher Acrylic Picture Varnish.

Dancing Dolphins

Grumbacher Acrylic Colors
Burnt Sienna
Grumbacher Payne's Gray
Grumbacher Purple (Dioxazine Purple)
Prussian Blue
Thalo® Blue
Thalo® Green (Blue Shade)
Ultramarine Blue
Yellow Ochre Light

Brushes
Two 2" Gesso Brushes
Gainsborough® #6 Flat Bristle Brush
½" Sable Essence™ Angle Brush
#1 Bristle Fan Brush
Golden Edge™ #2 liner Brush
Golden Edge™ #8 Filbert Brush

Other Supplies
16"x20" Stretched Canvas
Grumbacher Acrylic Painting Varnish
Whiteblend
Clearblend
Tapered Painting Knife
Toothbrush
Natural Sponge
Adhesive Design Protector
Tracing Paper
White Graphite Paper, Stylus

This is dedicated to CJ—Claudia Jennings Coleman. She created "Dancing Dolphins" and wanted to share them with you. CJ was a Koh-I-Noor Certified Artist, a talented artist, gifted teacher, and a dear friend. She was a joy to know. I love and miss her.

Palette
Before you begin, prepare these color mixtures:

Blue-Green—4 parts Prussian Blue, 1 part Thalo® Blue, 1 part Clearblend

Green-Blue—2 parts Thalo® Blue, 2 parts Thalo® Green, 2 parts Burnt Sienna, 1 part Clearblend

Navy—8 parts Ultramarine Blue, 2 parts Burnt Sienna, 1 part Grumbacher Purple

Teal—Whiteblend, Blue-Green

Seafoam—Whiteblend, Green-blue

Sky Blue—Whiteblend, Ultramarine Blue

Off-White—Whiteblend, touch of Yellow Ochre Light

1 **Background** (steps 1–4): Apply and blend the crest of the water wet-into-wet. Use a gesso brush to apply blue-green in the top left third and the bottom right third of the canvas. With the uncleaned brush, apply dashes of navy randomly into those areas. Paint the center with a clean brush loaded with green-blue, connecting the top left and bottom right areas of the canvas. Scrub around with the green-blue brush to blend the colors together.

1

2

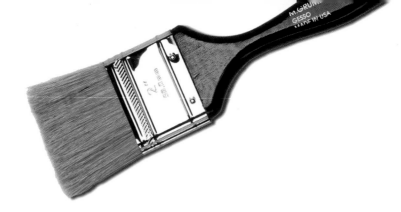

3

4

2 While the paint is wet, pick up Whiteblend on the uncleaned green-blue brush and zigzag an irregular S-shaped light area through the wet paint.

3 Use the uncleaned brush to pull down on both sides of the light area, indicating the direction of water movement.

4 While the paint is still wet, use Whiteblend on a flat bristle or fan brush to apply more movement and detail to the water; don't cover all the dark. Blend slightly with a clean towel-dried fan brush, leaving light and dark streaks. Dry.

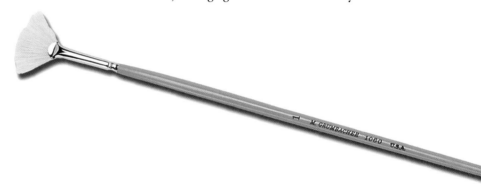

5

5 Transfer the dolphins to the canvas with white graphite paper. The baby dolphin's eye is 10½" from the top of the canvas and 8½" from the right side. Cut a design protector from the same pattern and attach it over the dolphins.

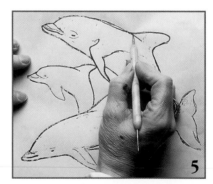

6

6 Use a clean gesso brush to cover the wave above the dolphins with Clearblend. With teal on a small section of the moist sponge, tap along the crest of the wave to create small splashes above and to the left of the dolphins.

7 Use a clean fan brush with Clearblend to pull the outer edges of the splashes down on either side of the wave, connecting them with the moving water.

8 Touch up the water by covering it with Clearblend, then adding the appropriate color. Blend while the color is wet, fading the edges. Dry.

9 Use a small area of the sponge to create the irregularly shaped splash behind the dolphins by lightly tapping contrasting colors onto the canvas. Alternate seafoam, teal and sky blue. Sponge mix the colors with Whiteblend to create differing values. Use different areas of the sponge or clean it between colors.

10 With a clean sponge and off-white, brighten areas of the splash, especially along the back of the dolphin.

11 Brush-mix ½ water and ½ paint from the splash. Load a toothbrush with these thinned colors, turn the bristles toward the canvas and scrape over the bristles with your finger or painting knife to flick tiny splatters of these colors in and around the splash. Repeat with a fan brush to flick larger splatters. Remove unwanted splatters with a clean moist sponge. Dry. Remove the design protector.

12 **Dolphins:** Paint, highlight and blend a small section of each dolphin at a time. With the angle brush, apply blue-green to the back and fin of the most distant dolphin. Add Whiteblend or sky blue to the uncleaned brush, paint the connecting subtle light area and blend.

13 Continue painting and blending until the dolphin's body is complete.

14 Use an angle brush to accent the mouth. Use a liner brush to add a dot of sky blue for the eye. Dry.

15 Paint each dolphin the same way. To touch up the dolphins, apply Clearblend first, then the color, then blend. Dry.

16 Use the liner brush to apply off-white on the most distant dolphin's head. Use the filbert or angle brush with Clearblend to fade the inner edge of the off-white. Repeat for the nose.

17 Add an off-white highlight to the top left eye. Draw a thin line of off-white highlight along the flipper. Repeat for all the dolphins. To tone down any excess light color, add blue-green and blend. Dry. Erase unwanted graphite marks with a clean moist sponge.

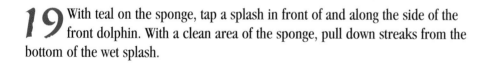

18 **Foreground:** Shield the foreground dolphin with a piece of paper as you add the middle splash between the dolphins with a sponge, using the colors and technique from steps 9–10. Use a clean moist angle brush to touch up the edge of the splash or remove excess from the dolphins.

19 With teal on the sponge, tap a splash in front of and along the side of the front dolphin. With a clean area of the sponge, pull down streaks from the bottom of the wet splash.

20 Add Whiteblend to the uncleaned sponge to create brighter splash colors in front of the dolphins. With a clean area of the sponge, apply off-white and pure Whiteblend splashes in the center of the large foreground splash.

21 Follow step 11 to flick specks of color around the foreground splash. Remove "uh-ohs" with a clean damp sponge. Dry.

Sign and "dance with your dolphins!" When the painting is dry, use a kneaded eraser or moist sponge to remove any excess graphite lines. Spray your completely dry painting with Grumbacher Acrylic Painting Varnish.

A Place to Ponder

Grumbacher Acrylic Colors
Burnt Sienna
Burnt Umber
Cadmium Yellow Medium
Grumbacher Payne's Gray
Monoazo Orange
Prussian Blue
Sap Green
Thalo® Crimson
Titanium White
Yellow Ochre Light

Brushes
2" Gesso Brush
2" Hake Brush
Gainsborough® #6 Flat Bristle Brush
Sable Essence™ ½" Angle Brush
#1 Bristle Fan Brush
Multi-Texture Brush

Other Supplies
16"x20" Stretched Canvas
Grumbacher Acrylic Painting Varnish
Whiteblend
Clearblend
Slowblend
Soft Lead Pencil
Tapered Painting Knife
Natural Sponge

Palette

Before you begin, prepare these color mixtures:

Peach—Whiteblend, touch of Monoazo Orange

Teal—Whiteblend, touch of Prussian Blue

Violet-Gray—Whiteblend, 1 part Grumbacher Gray, 1 part Prussian Blue, 1 part Thalo® Crimson

Dark Green—2 parts Grumbacher Gray, 2 parts Sap Green, 1 part Burnt Sienna

Gray-Green—2 parts Whiteblend, 1 part Violet-Gray, 1 part Dark Green

Sunny Yellow—10 parts Whiteblend, 1 part Cadmium Yellow Medium

1 **Canvas preparation:** Sketch a rough outline onto the canvas, placing the most distant water line 4" from the bottom, the crest of the most distant meadow 4¾" from the bottom, and the tallest mountain peak 9½" from the bottom of the canvas. Dampen the sky area with water and blot away any drips. **Sky:** Use the gesso brush with peach to paint from the top of the canvas to the horizon line. Wipe excess paint from the brush and apply teal in an irregular pattern around the top and sides of the canvas.

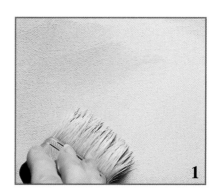

1

2 Wipe excess paint from the brush and blend the inner edges of the teal into the peach. Do the final blending with a hake brush.

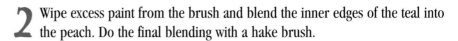

3 **Water:** With horizontal strokes of a clean gesso brush, apply peach in the top half of the water area. Use a flat bristle brush to apply teal along the bottom and sides. Add more Prussian Blue to the uncleaned brush and apply darker streaks in the bottom of the water. Blend using horizontal strokes and a clean, dry, gesso brush. Dry.

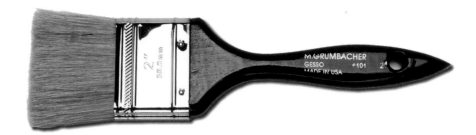

4 **Mountains:** Use a gesso brush to cover the mountains with Slowblend. While the Slowblend is wet, use a lightly-loaded painting knife to apply violet-gray over the tops of the left two mountains. Scrape the paint around, creating a thin coating.

5 To blend and create a mist around the mountain bases, hold a clean, dry gesso brush 45° off the canvas, handle angled down, and tap around in the bottom of the wet violet-gray and Slowblend, gradually fading the color toward the meadow.

6 Create a lighter value of violet-gray by adding Whiteblend to some of the violet-gray on the painting knife. Apply the lightened gray to the distant mountain. Pat to blend the bottom edges of the wet gray paint with the gesso brush as described in Step 5.

7 While the mountains are still wet, load the painting knife with marbleized peach to apply highlights on the left sides of the ridges. Apply as little as pressure as possible as you drag the knife, allowing the paint to skip over the surface, leaving breaks and craters on the mountain. Use the painting knife to apply reflected lights of marbleized teal on the right sides. Using the fan brush, pat and blend the bottoms of these wet colors down gradually as before.

8 Touch up unwanted ragged edges along the mountain peaks with the angle brush and the appropriate color for that area.

9 **Distant trees:** Load a clean fan brush with gray-green to paint the distant foliage and trees. Paint irregular sizes and shapes. Hold your brush vertically for taller trees.

10 **Meadow:** Use the fan brush to apply dark green across the bottom of the meadow along the waterline. Load a clean fan brush with sunny yellow, hold the brush about 45° off the canvas, handle pointing down, and tap to apply grass at the crest. Continue tapping the sunny yellow brush around so it connects to the wet dark green and creates a middle-value green in the center. Clean the brush thoroughly and pat to blend any areas that need touching up.

11 Load dark green onto a clean fan brush to create irregular sizes and shapes of foliage on the right side of the canvas. **Evergreens:** With the brush turned vertically, tap lightly to create a tree top. Turn the brush horizontally and tap lightly with a corner to create branches. Zigzag the limbs in an irregular pattern, making them wider, larger and denser as you paint toward the bottom of the tree.

12 Use the same colors to add a bush on the right side.

13 Add Yellow Ochre Light and a touch of Whiteblend to the uncleaned fan brush. Lightly pat highlights on the top and left sides of the branches. Add more Yellow Ochre Light and a touch of sunny yellow to the uncleaned brush and randomly brighten the top edges of a few highlighted areas. Use the flat bristle brush to crunch the same highlight colors around in the remaining foliage. Add teal to the uncleaned brush to add reflected light on the right sides of the foliage and trees.

14 **Reflections:** With a clean gesso brush, cover the water area under the foliage and along the water edge with Slowblend. Paint and blend the reflections wet-into-wet. Using a fan brush with dark green, stroke down to reflect the grass and pat around with the brush to create a reflection resembling the foliage directly underneath it.

15 With a light touch of the hake brush, lightly brush down over the reflections. Towel-clean the brush. To create a shimmer, alternate stroking the wet reflection horizontally to the right and to the left. Hold the brush horizontally, stroke across the reflection, clean the brush and place it adjacent to the previous stroke to brush across the reflection from the opposite direction. Repeat as needed.

16 **Bank:** Load a flat bristle brush with Burnt Umber. Use horizontal strokes to paint a bank between the trees and the reflection. With a clean flat bristle brush, apply brush-mixed highlights of Whiteblend, Monoazo Orange and Yellow Ochre Light to the bank; do not overblend. Add more Whiteblend to the brush to highlight some of the rocks.

17 Apply the dark green center island foliage with a flat bristle brush. Hold the brush perpendicular to the canvas and crunch upward.

18 Brush-mix Yellow Ochre Light and Whiteblend onto the uncleaned brush and tap highlights on the top and right sides of the foliage clusters. Add Yellow Ochre Light, Cadmium Yellow Medium and Titanium White to brighten the top edges of the highlighted areas. Create reflections as before. With the fan brush and dark green, stroke upward along the island edge to create grass; stroke down to reflect it.

19 Apply and highlight the left foliage, then create reflections as before. Dry. With a clean flat bristle brush, tap Monoazo Orange shrubs randomly in the foliage. Blot the bottom of the wet orange paint with your finger to "plant" it.

20 Wet the reflections with Clearblend. Tap a dab of Monoazo Orange in the reflection below where it appears in the foliage. Randomly tap a hint of the highlight colors in some areas. Shimmer as before; dry. Apply waterlines with the painting knife., using teal in the shadow areas of the reflection and Titanium White in the light areas. Use a clean fan brush moistened with Clearblend to soften the waterlines by brushing horizontally along the edges.

21 Brush-mix a watery combination of violet-gray and Grumbacher Gray with the liner brush. Add tiny birds.

Sign. Sit back and ponder. When the canvas is dry, use a kneaded eraser or damp sponge to remove excess pencil lines. Spray your thoroughly dry painting with Grumbacher Acrylic Painting Varnish.

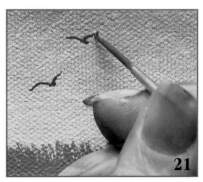

Anchors Aweigh

Grumbacher Acrylic Colors
Burnt Sienna
Burnt Umber
Iridescent White
Monoazo Orange
Thalo® Copper
Thalo® Green (Blue Shade)
Thio™ Violet (Quinacridone Magenta)
Titanium White
Ultramarine Blue
Yellow Ochre Light

Brushes
Two 2" Gesso Brushes
Gainsborough® #6 Flat Bristle Brush
Golden Edge™ #8 Filbert Brush
Sable Essence™ ½" Angle Brush
Golden Edge™ #2 Liner Brush
#1 Bristle Fan Brush
Multi-Texture Brush

Other Supplies
16"x20" Stretched Canvas
Grumbacher Acrylic Painting Varnish
Whiteblend
Clearblend
Grumbacher Modeling Paste
Tapered Painting Knife
Natural Sponge
Plastic Fork
Toothbrush
Black Graphite Paper, Stylus

Palette

Before you begin, prepare these color mixtures:

Medium Blue-Gray—4 parts Whiteblend, 1 part Ultramarine Blue, touch of Burnt Umber

Light Blue-Gray—1 part Medium Blue-Gray, 1 part Whiteblend

Seafoam—15 parts Whiteblend, 1 part Thalo® Green, touch of Ultramarine Blue

Terra Cotta—6 parts Whiteblend, 1 part Burnt Sienna

Tan—6 parts Whiteblend, 1 part Burnt Umber

Peach—Whiteblend, touch of Monoazo Orange

Violet-Gray—Medium Blue-Gray, touch of Thio™ Violet

Maroon—Burnt Umber, touch of Thio™ Violet, touch of Ultramarine Blue

Shadow—4 parts Ultramarine Blue, 1 part Monoazo Orange, 3 parts Clearblend

1 **Canvas preparation:** Transfer the pattern to the canvas, placing the center of the anchor crosspiece 6" from the bottom of the canvas and 10" from the left side. With a painting knife, pile modeling paste on the rope and anchor—just "glob" the paste on.

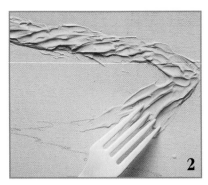

2 To create texture, drag and pat around in the wet paste with the painting knife. Use a plastic fork to create the frayed ends of the rope. Allow it to dry overnight.

3 **Base coat:** Use horizontal strokes of the gesso brushes to apply and blend the water and sand areas. Apply streaks of seafoam through all the water areas. With the uncleaned brush, add horizontal streaks of light blue-gray in the top water section, streaks of medium blue-gray in the bottom, and a mixture of both in the center. With a clean gesso brush, apply Whiteblend along the edges of the water and blend to gradually fade the color. Set this Whiteblend brush aside for the next step.

4 With a clean gesso brush, apply streaks of terra cotta and tan through the centers of the sand areas. Add Burnt Umber, Ultramarine Blue, Burnt Sienna and maroon to the uncleaned brush and darken the beach in the bottom right corner, around the anchor and its attached rope. If the colors are too dark, add Whiteblend to the uncleaned brush. Blend the water and sand areas together with the Whiteblend brush from step 2, creating a gradual transition. Dry.

5 **Water and sand:** Cover the top half of the canvas with Clearblend. While it is wet, use Whiteblend on the painting knife to apply the top tide line.

6 Blend the top edges of the Whiteblend by brushing horizontally, back and forth, gradually moving upward. Repeat this technique to add all the tide lines and streaks in the water.

7 While each area is still wet with Clearblend, use a fan brush to brush-mix Whiteblend with a touch of Yellow Ochre Light and add accents in the sand. Blend. Dry the canvas thoroughly.

8 Apply Clearblend to the ground under the ropes and anchor, then use the angle brush to apply shadow in these wet areas. Work one section at a time. Blend with a clean fan brush moistened with Clearblend. Clean the blending brush often. Dry.

9 **Anchor and rope:** Use the flat bristle brush to paint the anchor, alternating Burnt Umber and Burnt Sienna. Paint the rope attached to the anchor Burnt Umber. Add a touch of Whiteblend to the Burnt Umber in the brush for the distant rope. Dry. Before adding details, touch up any areas by covering the area with Clearblend first, then adding light colors or dark shadows across the sand, emphasizing them as needed, especially in the bottom right corner of the canvas. Blend and dry.

10 Double load the angle brush so that as you paint, the bottom dispenses Burnt Umber and the top peach. Place the brush on the front rope and drag it in a slight arch over the rope. Repeat, creating a twisted, three-dimensional appearance. Add a touch of tan to the Burnt Umber in the brush for the distant rope. Use the angle brush or liner to make streaks of both light and dark colors on the frayed ends.

11 With the Multi-Texture brush, alternate using Burnt Umber, Burnt Sienna and Monoazo Orange to paint the rust on the anchor.

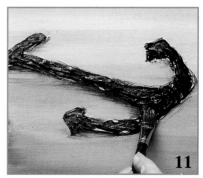

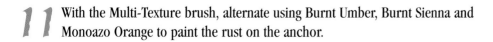

12 Use the same brush and colors to lift ragged spikes of rust off the anchor.

13 Load a dry flat bristle brush with a mixture of Monoazo Orange, a touch of Burnt Sienna and Titanium White. Lightly tap to highlight the ridges along the top of the anchor. Add more Monoazo Orange, a touch of Yellow Ochre and Titanium White to the uncleaned brush and repeat.

14 Load the liner brush with maroon to paint a circular end on the crosspiece of the anchor and to touch up the shadows along the bottom edges. Pat the inner edges of the wet shadow color with a clean towel-dried flat bristle brush to create a gradual but uneven transition. Dry.

15 With a clean, dry flat bristle brush, dabble Thalo® Copper randomly on the top portions of the anchor. Dabble a few spots of Iridescent White to indicate shiny wet spots.

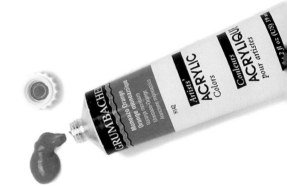

16 With the liner brush and water colors, apply a broken line of reflected light along the anchor bottom, separating it from its shadow on the sand. Dry.

17 **Sand details:** Use the flat bristle brush to pile peach and tan on areas of the anchor, "burying" parts of it in the sand. Use a clean flat bristle brush moistened with Clearblend to soften and fade the bottom edges of the wet paint horizontally away from the anchor over the dry sand.

18 With violet-gray and a variety of brush-mixed colors on the filbert brush, apply C-strokes resembling oyster shells on the beach around the anchor. Apply these in different sizes, overlapping some. While they are wet, use a clean filbert brush with Whiteblend to stroke through the centers of the shells, creating the concave pearlized interiors. Now reverse the colors. Apply Whiteblend first, then dark centers. Repeat, but with lighter values, on the distant sand.

19 Double load the angle brush with dark on the bottom and light on the top. Tap around in the foreground to create clusters of irregularly shaped shells. Use a variety of colors from your palette. Blot the bottoms while wet to "plant" them. Use lighter values in the distant sand.

20 Be creative! Use a filbert brush loaded with light and dark colors to create any shell or "do-for" that you might find washed up on the beach. When dry, use the liner brush and shadow mixture to add zigzag shadows along the right sides and under some shells. Blot the bottoms of the shadows with a filbert brush to create a soft transition.

21 **Bubbles:** Use the liner brush and Whiteblend thinned slightly with a touch of water to draw circles for the small bubbles. While they are wet, use a filbert brush moistened with Clearblend to soften the inner edges. Use the liner brush and medium blue-gray to apply a C-stroke inside the bottom right portion of each bubble; soften with the filbert brush. Add a Whiteblend catchlight dot inside the top left portion of the bubble. For large bubbles, apply Clearblend first, then circle it with Whiteblend; proceed as before. For tiny bubbles, do not blend the inside edges. Add lots of bubbles of all sizes and shapes. Dry. Touch up as needed.

22 Speckle your painting with any and all colors from the palette, including Whiteblend. Thin the colors to the consistency of whole milk. Load a fan or toothbrush with the thinned color, turn the bristles toward the canvas and scrape over the bristles with your finger or a painting knife; flick speckles randomly around. Remove any unwanted speckles with a clean moist sponge. Dry.

Sign and sing, "Anchors aweigh, my friends, anchors aweigh!" When your painting is thoroughly dry, use a kneaded eraser or damp sponge to remove excess graphite lines. Spray with Grumbacher Acrylic Painting Varnish.

Jewel of the Sky

Grumbacher Acrylic Colors
Burnt Sienna
Grumbacher Payne's Gray
Grumbacher Purple (Dioxazine Purple)
Grumbacher Red (Naphthol Red)
Hooker's Green
Interference Blue
Interference Green
Interference Red
Interference Violet
Monoazo Orange
Thalo® Crimson
Thalo® Yellow Green
Ultramarine Blue
Yellow Ochre Light

Brushes
Two 2" Gesso Brushes
2" Hake Brush
Golden Edge™ #2 Liner Brush
Sable Essence™ ½" Angle Brush
Golden Edge™ #6 Round Brush
Multi-Texture Brush
#1 Bristle Fan Brush

Other Supplies
16"x20" Stretched Canvas
Grumbacher Acrylic Painting Varnish
Whiteblend
Clearblend
Tapered Painting Knife
Natural Sponge
Black Graphite Paper
Stylus

Palette

Before you begin, prepare these color mixtures:

Off-White—Whiteblend, touch of Yellow Ochre Light (mix about 3 tablespoons)

Pink—Whiteblend, touch of Grumbacher Red

Peach—Whiteblend, touch of Monoazo Orange

Navy—1 part Grumbacher Gray, 1 part Ultramarine Blue

Blue-Green—1 part Ultramarine Blue, 1 part Hooker's Green

Yellow-Green—1 part Blue-Green, 1 part Thalo® Yellow Green

Light Green—Blue-Green, Whiteblend

Taupe—2 parts Whiteblend, 2 parts Grumbacher Gray, 1 part Monoazo Orange

Light Taupe—Taupe, Whiteblend

Violet-Gray—Whiteblend, touch of Navy, smaller touch of Grumbacher Purple

Light Blue—Whiteblend, touch of Ultramarine Blue

1 **Background:** Apply and blend the background wet-into-wet. To extend the drying time, first dampen the canvas with water and blot excess runs or drips. Use a gesso brush to generously cover the canvas with off-white. Wipe excess paint from the brush and use it to apply dashes of navy, blue-green, and yellow-green randomly around the canvas, avoiding the center and wiping off excess paint between colors. Use a fan brush to apply dashes of pink and peach in the center area. Blend with a clean towel-dried gesso brush using figure-8 or X-strokes. Clean the brush frequently while you blend. Complete the final blending with the hake, using a feather touch and an erratic motion. Dry. Transfer the design, placing the bird's eye 7½" from the top edge and 9" from the right side of the canvas.

1

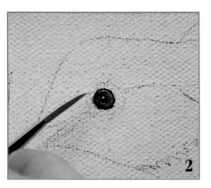

2 **Hummingbird:** Use the round or liner brush to paint the eye Burnt Sienna. Dry. Add a round Grumbacher Gray pupil in the center of the eye, and a thin broken outline of Grumbacher Gray around the eye. Dry. Add a tiny Whiteblend dot for a catchlight on the top left pupil.

3 Leave an irregular unpainted space around the eye as you paint the Grumbacher Gray marking around it and on the head.

4 Use a small round brush loaded with Grumbacher Gray to paint the beak. Draw a peach line to separate the top and bottom of the beak.

5 Use a clean angle brush to paint the bottom of his tail Grumbacher Gray.

6 Paint the top of his head blue-green.

7

8

9

7 Use the angle brush to paint the ruby throat with a progression of connecting colors: Start at the top with Monoazo Orange, add Grumbacher Red, then Thalo® Crimson, and end with Grumbacher Purple along the bottom and right. Gently wipe excess paint from the brush between colors. Blend with a clean, towel-dried angle brush moistened with Clearblend, tapping the brush where the colors join.

8 Load the angle brush with light taupe to paint the primary wing feathers. Add taupe to the brush for the other wing feathers.

9 Use the angle brush to draw streaks of taupe along the wet primary feathers, separating them. With the liner brush, add a touch more Monoazo Orange to peach and paint the top edge of each wing.

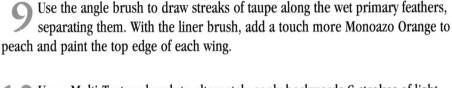
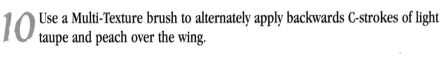

10 Use a Multi-Texture brush to alternately apply backwards C-strokes of light taupe and peach over the wing.

11 Paint his back with the angle brush, beginning with zig-zag strips of navy and a touch of Whiteblend.

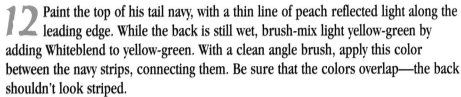
10

12 Paint the top of his tail navy, with a thin line of peach reflected light along the leading edge. While the back is still wet, brush-mix light yellow-green by adding Whiteblend to yellow-green. With a clean angle brush, apply this color between the navy strips, connecting them. Be sure that the colors overlap—the back shouldn't look striped.

11

13 Alternate light blue and violet-gray to paint the shadows along his tummy and on his sit-upon. Apply Whiteblend in the center of the tummy and tap with a clean, towel-dried brush to pat-blend, leaving feathery markings. Dry.

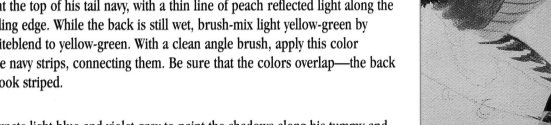

12

13

14 Use the Multi-Texture brush with a variety of greens from your palette to apply feathers on the top of his back wing, connecting the wings to the body, and under his front wing, overlapping his side and connecting to his back. Fade the green color onto the wings. Dry.

15 Use the Multi-Texture brush to highlight the feather markings—use Thalo® Yellow Green and a touch of Whiteblend on the head, painting with C-strokes and blotting with your finger along the edges to create a rounded appearance. Add Monoazo Orange with a touch of Whiteblend on the center of the ruby throat. Dry and blot the outer edges as before.

16 Use watery Grumbacher Gray on the small round or liner brush to paint his feet and legs.

17 Touch up the dark facial marking, extending it under the wing. Load a clean moist Multi-Texture brush with Clearblend and soften the marking under the wing. Use a liner brush to touch up any other areas. Use a lightly loaded Multi-Texture brush and C-strokes to apply sparse, iridescent sparkles of the Interference colors on the bird, rinsing the brush between colors. Apply Interference Green on the green areas, Interference Red on the ruby throat, Interference Violet on his sit-upon and the shadowy areas of the throat. Add dabbles of Interference Blue on his back and a few tiny touches on his head, wings and tail.

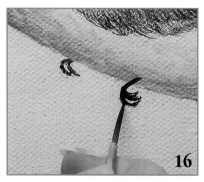

18 Distant foliage: On the liner brush, double load peach alternately with light green or light taupe to create the limbs. Blot the origination points of the limbs, making them fade into the background.

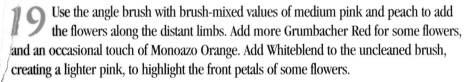

19 Use the angle brush with brush-mixed values of medium pink and peach to add the flowers along the distant limbs. Add more Grumbacher Red for some flowers, and an occasional touch of Monoazo Orange. Add Whiteblend to the uncleaned brush, creating a lighter pink, to highlight the front petals of some flowers.

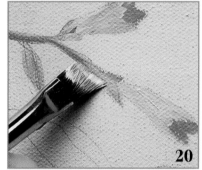

20 With a clean angle brush, add leaves along the branches and light green calices at the flower bases. Dry.

21 Foreground foliage: Use the angle brush to apply the foreground limb, leaves and flowers in the same way as the distant ones, but use darker color values and apply more pressure on the brushes, making the foreground objects darker, larger, and lower on the canvas. Alternate dark and light values of pink and peach, giving more detail to the larger blooms.

22 Double load blue-green and light green to paint the foreground leaves. Use an angle brush to shadow parts of some with blue-green, making them appear tilted and bent. When dry, add detail lines on some leaves with the liner brush and a contrasting value of blue-green.

23 Use the round brush and the same colors to add tiny buds and leaves at the tip of the limb. Dry.

Sign…and hummm. After the painting is dry, remove excess graphite marks with a damp sponge or kneaded eraser. A few days later, spray it with Grumbacher Acrylic Painting Varnish.

Flurries on the Farm

Grumbacher Acrylic Colors
Burnt Umber
Monoazo Orange
Titanium White
Ultramarine Blue

Brushes
2" Gesso Brush
2" Hake Brush
#1 Bristle Fan Brush
Multi-Texture Brush
Golden Edge™ #2 Liner Brush
Golden Edge™ #6 Flat Detail Brush
Gainsborough® #6 Flat Bristle Brush
½" Sable Essence™ Angle Brush

Other Supplies
16"x20" stretched canvas
Grumbacher Acrylic Painting Varnish
Clearblend
Whiteblend
Matte Medium & Varnish
Tapered Painting Knife
Natural Sponge
Rapidograph Technical Pen #2.00
Rotring Artist's Ink: Brown
16"x20" Mat Template
(11½"x15½" opening)
Masking Tape, Scissors
Adhesive Design Protector
Black Graphite Paper, Stylus

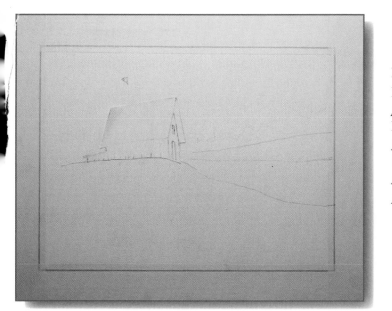

Palette
Before you begin, prepare these color mixtures:

Medium Violet-Gray—Whiteblend, 3 parts Ultramarine Blue, 1 part Monoazo Orange

Light Violet-Gray—2 parts Medium violet-gray, 1 part Whiteblend

Pale Peach—Whiteblend, touch of Monoazo Orange

Light Blue—6 parts Whiteblend, 1 part Ultramarine Blue

1 **Canvas preparation:** Transfer the design so the front roof peak is 5" from the top and 9" from the left edge of the canvas. Transfer the barn onto the adhesive design protector, cut it out and place it securely over the barn on the canvas. Place the canvas face up on a flat surface. Align the mat template with the canvas edges. Hold it securely in place while you use the pen to slowly draw a line along the inside edges of the opening. Repeat if the line is irregular. Dry the canvas thoroughly.

2 Place masking tape over each side of the rectangular marking so it extends ³⁄₈" inside the marked line. Use a gesso or fan brush to seal the inner edges of the tape and the outer edges of the design protector with Matte Medium. Dry.

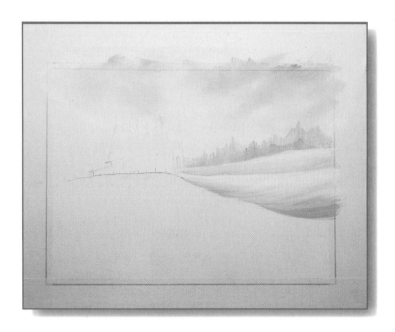

3 **Sky:** Paint the sky wet-into-wet. Load the gesso brush with Whiteblend and cover the sky area. Wipe any excess Whiteblend off your brush. Use the same brush to apply pale peach along the horizon. Add drifting streaks of light violet-gray and light blue coming down from the top of the wet sky.

4 Blend with light pressure and erratic strokes, using a dry hake brush to create a blustery sky. Continue to step 5 while the sky is still wet.

5 **Distant trees:** With the fan brush, mix a variety of values by alternately adding small amounts of Whiteblend, pale peach or Burnt Umber to light violet-gray. Begin with the lightest colors, gradually adding darker values as you paint. Hold the brush vertically and stroke downward to create the illusion of distant trees along the horizon. Create smaller trees by holding the brush horizontally. Change the value of the violet-gray occasionally and notice how darker colors come forward and lighter values recede. Use a clean moist sponge to wipe excess tree paint off the hillside.

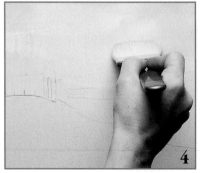

6 **Distant meadows:** Use the fan brush to apply Whiteblend on the top of the distant meadow. Add violet-gray and a touch of Whiteblend to the uncleaned brush and paint the valley of the same meadow, just above the line indicating the top of the middle meadow. Blend the violet-gray up into the bottom of the Whiteblend. Blend with a clean towel-dried fan brush, giving direction to the snowdrifts with the brush strokes; do not overblend.

7 With a clean fan brush, apply Whiteblend in the top of the middle meadow. Paint the valley and remaining middle meadow violet-gray. Add pale peach to the uncleaned brush and apply a few accents. Blend as before with a clean towel-dried fan brush, leaving the middle meadow one value darker than the more distant one. Dry.

8 **Foreground trees:** Brush-mix Burnt Umber and water to the consistency of Whiteblend, making creamy Burnt Umber. Load a painting knife or fan brush and begin applying this to the edges of the design protector, stroking away from it. Scrub the color around erratically to create streaks. Add dabs of Monoazo Orange randomly in the wet Burnt Umber. Tap over the wet tree colors with a clean, moist, squeezed-dry sponge to create leaf texture and irregular, lacy outer edges.

9 Load the fan brush with creamy Burnt Umber mixed with a touch of Monoazo Orange. Hold the brush vertically and use the corner to tap a small bush in front of the barn. Use a clean area of the moist sponge to wipe the foliage paint off the snow at the crest of the hill.

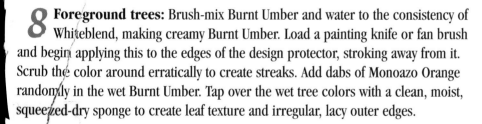

10 **Foreground meadow:** Load the gesso brush with medium violet-gray and paint the bottom half of the meadow. Use a clean brush to apply Whiteblend along the top of the hill, overlapping the medium violet-gray. With a fan brush, add streaks of light blue or pale peach to the crest of the meadow for accents.

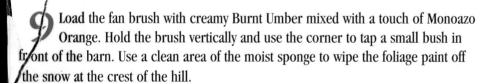

11 Emphasize the lay of the land by stroking a clean towel-dried fan brush across the meadow, creating dark and light drifts in the snow. Determine the slope of the snow bank with the direction of the brush strokes. Do not overblend. Dry the canvas thoroughly.

12 **Barn:** Remove the design protector. Use the angle brush to apply Whiteblend to the top two-thirds of the barn roof. Load your uncleaned brush with light violet-gray and stroke upward from the bottom edge of the roof, over the Whiteblend. Follow the slope of the roof with each stroke. Blend with a clean, towel-dried angle brush.

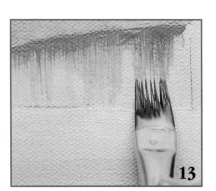

13 Brush-mix a touch of Burnt Umber with medium violet-gray to create tan-gray. Use the angle brush with this mixture to paint a shadow under the roof on the side of the barn. While the shadow is still wet, load a Multi-Texture brush with Clearblend and stroke downward from the bottom of the tan-gray paint, pulling streaks of color over the side of the barn to indicate weathered wood. Add light blue to the angle brush to define the front corner of the barn. Stroke vertically with the Multi-Texture brush, gradually moving the inner part of the corner shadow over the barn.

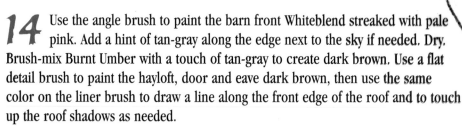

14 Use the angle brush to paint the barn front Whiteblend streaked with pale pink. Add a hint of tan-gray along the edge next to the sky if needed. Dry. Brush-mix Burnt Umber with a touch of tan-gray to create dark brown. Use a flat detail brush to paint the hayloft, door and eave dark brown, then use the same color on the liner brush to draw a line along the front edge of the roof and to touch up the roof shadows as needed.

15 Use the angle brush to pile Titanium White along the top of the roof. Use a clean angle brush moistened with Clearblend to pull the bottom edges of the wet paint down over the roof paint. Use the liner brush with Whiteblend to draw roof lines on top of the back shed and along the front eaves. Dry.